# Modern Origami

*by*

## JAMES MINORU SAKODA

A Fireside Book
Published by
Simon and Schuster

ISBN 0-671-20355-X
Library of Congress Catalog Card Number 77-84130
Designed by Libra Studios, Inc.
Manufactured in the United States of America

5   6   7   8   9   10   11   12   13

# Preface

During the past fifteen years or so I have spent many hours folding square pieces of paper into animals, flowers and human figures. I have done this on trains and airplanes, at meetings and parties, and particularly in the evening while pretending to watch television. During that time I have developed well over a hundred original figures, many of which my friends have admired for elegance of design, three-dimensional quality, the sheer intricacy of the folds involved, or just plain cuteness. From time to time I have jotted down sketches for the steps of a few of the figures and put them in a "diary." But most of these were only reminders to myself and could hardly be used by others. I have also tried to teach some of the figures to some of the secretaries I have had, to my son, Bill, to a few friends, to folders who gathered at the annual origami convention sponsored by Mrs. Lillian Oppenheimer at the Origami Center in New York City. Without written instructions, however, it has been a losing battle against the erosion of memory. Most of the figures, taught with difficulty, are forgotten within a matter of days, weeks or months. I have been fearful that the designs which I have developed will be lost, as countless others must have been. Some of them now will be preserved as written instructions, providing opportunities for others to learn them.

I owe special thanks to Anneliese Greenier for work on drawings for the "Origami Diary," and to Eileen Kelly for some initial help on this project. For this book I had to give up the idea of having others do the drawings for me; for they had left for other parts and there was no one to whom I could turn over the tedious task. I am thankful to the saleslady at Oaks-on-the-Hill in Providence, Rhode Island, who introduced me to the Mars pens, without which I could not have made acceptable ink drawings. To Bill, my son, I owe the designs for the cow and the lion and the technical assistance on the photographs.

I have also been greatly encouraged in the project by a number of friends, including Mr. and Mrs. Rolf Larson and their children, Dick, Kris, Amy and Janet, who served as official guinea pigs for the instructions as they were developed. They were new to origami, but their response to the written instructions I sent them was gratifying and encouraged me to complete the book. I would also like to thank more experienced folders who tested out the instructions and made valuable suggestions for improvement. They include Rae Cooker, Raymond McLain, Jessie Seto and Herman Shall. I thank Rheta Martin for general assistance and the typing of the manuscript. I am also grateful to the Department of Sociology and Anthropology of Brown University for permitting me to indulge in my non-scholarly activity.

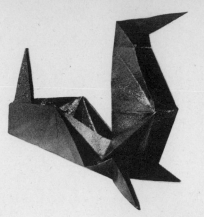

# Contents

To cherry blossoms I come,
    And under the blossoms go to sleep—
    No duties to be done!
                        —BUSON

# CHAPTER I

# An Introduction to Modern Origami

**THE NATURE OF THE BOOK**

A common criticism of beginner's origami books is that the directions are difficult to follow, and when one succeeds in finishing an object it is not terribly exciting or attractive. One might start with a paper cup, go on to a boat or a ball (known as a water bomb to those who have attended college and have had occasion to drop them on fellow students) and end up, if fortunate, with a successfully folded sitting crane or even a frog. More often than not the child is unable to do the squash fold for the square preliminary fold or the base for the sitting crane. He runs to his parents, who give it a cursory try and then give up, and the origami book, probably received for Christmas or as a birthday present, is put away in favor of more satisfying articles. A basic source of difficulty is the belief that origami is a childish pastime and therefore not worth much effort. Still another is the desire to skip the preliminary lessons and plunge into the middle.

It is my belief that this book will be more successful where others have failed. It is directed toward adult paper folding, which leads to more complex but also more satisfying creations than those found in books devoted to more traditional paper folding. It pays particular attention to systematic teaching of basic symbols and the manner in which instructions should be followed. The chapters which follow are generally arranged in order of difficulty. Each chapter is grouped around a basic fold such as bird base, eight-point star, T-fold, owl base, frog base, etc., so that several objects emerge from a single basic design. The directions are still not always easy to follow, even given the written instructions, the broken lines and the arrows, the result shown in a subsequent drawing, and, finally, a photograph of the finished object. Part of the lesson to be learned is that such directions are inherently difficult to write and even more difficult to follow; it is necessary to proceed chapter by chapter, step by step, and persevere when a hangup occurs. On the other hand, when a finished product is reached it can be a thing of beauty which is a source of endless pleasure. It provides entrance into a world of delightful make-believe, which one can enjoy alone or share with others.

## THE HISTORY OF ORIGAMI

*Origami* is a Japanese word for paper folding (*ori*, fold; *kami*, paper, which becomes *gami* when combined) and refers to the art of folding objects from a sheet of paper. *Origami* also refers to the use of folded paper for ceremonial use, such as the decorative *noshi* (see page 11) attached to gifts. Today the word *origami* is taken to mean folding of paper for pleasure rather than for any particular or ceremonial purpose. In Japan origami is a form of play, primarily for little girls. In its traditional form origami consists of folding square pieces of paper and making objects without cutting or pasting. Colored papers ranging in size from five to nine inches square are available commercially. The traditional figures include the helmet (*kabuto*), the double boat (*nisobune*), the inside-out boat (*fune*), the doll (*yakkosan*) and the popular and elegant sitting crane (*tsuru*), all shown on page 11. These figures are relatively simple in form, a result probably of the basic mode of transmission of knowledge from mother to child, with the aid of books written for children. Most traditional figures are flat rather than three-dimensional, boxy in form rather than long and elegant, and not particularly attractive as decorative objects. An exception is the sitting crane, which is the favorite among the Japanese. Its narrow head and tail, the clean-cut lines, and its three-dimensional form all combine to make it an attractive figure.

It is not clear just how ancient the art of origami for pleasure is. It is possible that it began in China and was brought to Japan, but this is just a conjecture. The existence of a Chinese junk (page 43) among the traditional folds leads one to suspect that paper folding was developed, at least in part, in China. It is not a popular folding in Japan, and Honda, who has a version of it in his book, refers to it as a

# TRADITIONAL ORIGAMI FIGURES

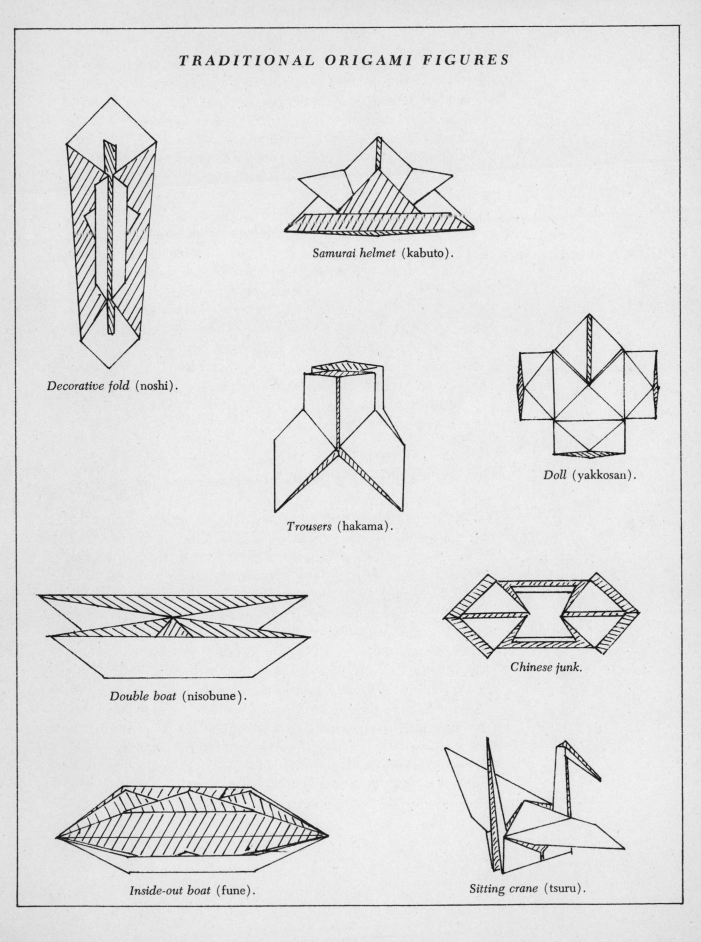

Decorative fold (noshi).

Samurai helmet (kabuto).

Doll (yakkosan).

Trousers (hakama).

Double boat (nisobune).

Chinese junk.

Inside-out boat (fune).

Sitting crane (tsuru).

Korean boat. According to Kosho Uchiyama, literary references clearly show that by the middle of the Edo Period (1614–1868) origami had become a popular pastime in Japan. The earliest definite citation is from a work published in 1682, in which reference is made to a seven-year-old child playing *orisue* (as origami was called) and making birds and flowers. He cites other references to the folding of the crane, the helmet and the double boat, indicating that these were in existence during that period.

In addition to origami for children, there also existed creative origami by adults. There is one reference by a writer who died in 1856 to a remarkable merchant in the Asakusa section of Tokyo who by folding paper could make any kind of human, animal and bird figures desired. A more tangible record of creative adult origami is Volume 233 of the encyclopedia *Kan no mado*. It was lost at one point, but a copy was recently discovered and published. It contains instructions for making complex figures such as the human figures, a dragonfly, a spider with eight legs, a lobster and Japanese dolls. The complexity is achieved in part by freely cutting around or into the paper. The book is undated, but is believed to have been published in the middle of the 1800s.

## THE RISE OF CREATIVE ADULT FOLDING

Since the end of World War II there has been a revival of interest in creative adult paper folding. An outstanding event was the publication of *Bibliography of Paper-Folding* by Gershon Legman in 1952. This was followed by the establishment of the Origami Center under the leadership of Lillian Oppenheimer. It held its first meeting in October 1958 and published the first issue of the *Origamian* the same year. The Origami Center has been instrumental in bringing adults interested in origami into contact with one another. Names featured in the *Origamian* include Akira Yosizawa from Japan, Ligia Montoya from Argentina, Robert Harbin from England, Peppino Baggi from Italy, Adolfo Cerceda from Buenos Aires, Fred Rohm from the United States, Michio and Kosho Uchiyama from Japan, Dr. Vincente Solorzano Sagredo from Spain. The author was featured in the winter 1964 edition. Several folders' groups have since been formed in various places, such as Argentina, England, and Japan, an indication of rising interest in adult paper folding. Some of the contributions of these folders and others have appeared in print and can be examined and learned at close hand. Particularly significant are Randlett's

*The Best of Origami* and Harbin's *Secrets of Origami,* both of which are collections of creative folds.

Each folder has a style of his own and has a unique contribution to make, if he is creative. The chief effort, of course, is to make original figures. Three special devices used to accomplish this are cutting the paper, pasting two folded pieces together, and starting from nonsquare forms such as a triangle, a rectangle, a hexagon, etc. On page 14 Adolfo Cerceda's lion is folded from two pieces, both from the widely used bird base. The dragonfly from the *Kan no mado* was folded from a square, but cuts were introduced to form the four wings. There is now a general tendency among the better folders to frown upon cutting or pasting, but these are considered permissible if the result is superb. Folding from forms other than a square, while not traditional, is generally considered permissible, Robert Harbin's attractive bat is folded from an equilateral triangle.

New figures can and have been made by clever innovators without recourse to pasting and cutting. Two distinctive approaches can be recognized. One is the systematic search for new basic folds from which a number of figures can be made. Outstanding exponents of this approach are Kosho Uchiyama and Dr. Vincente Solorzano Sagredo, both of whom have published books to their credit. For example, Uchiyama points out that the base for an eight-point figure can be made by putting together four sets of creases from a bird base, and that similarly the base for a twelve-point figure needed for the crab can be made from four sets of creases from the frog base. The unsystematic folder aims for an object and finds ways and means of arriving at it without particular concern for basic folds. A good example of this type of folder is Fred Rohm, who considers paper folding a challenge toward folding seemingly impossible combinations. His magic rabbit in a cube and his jack-in-the-box are good examples. The advantage of the systematic approach is that it provides for systematic accumulation of knowledge of related basic forms, and makes for easier teaching.

Another distinction can be made among folders on the basis of the appearance of the finished product rather than the complexity of the folds. Many folders strive for realism, putting in crooks in the legs and arms, rounding off corners, etc. The artistic folder, best illustrated by Ligia Montoya, observes the limitations of the paper, emphasizes clean-cut straight lines, which are characteristic of folds, and produces beautiful and somewhat stylized figures. Ligia Montoya used thin airmail paper, which helped to preserve clean-cut

## CONTRASTS IN STYLES OF ADULT FOLDERS

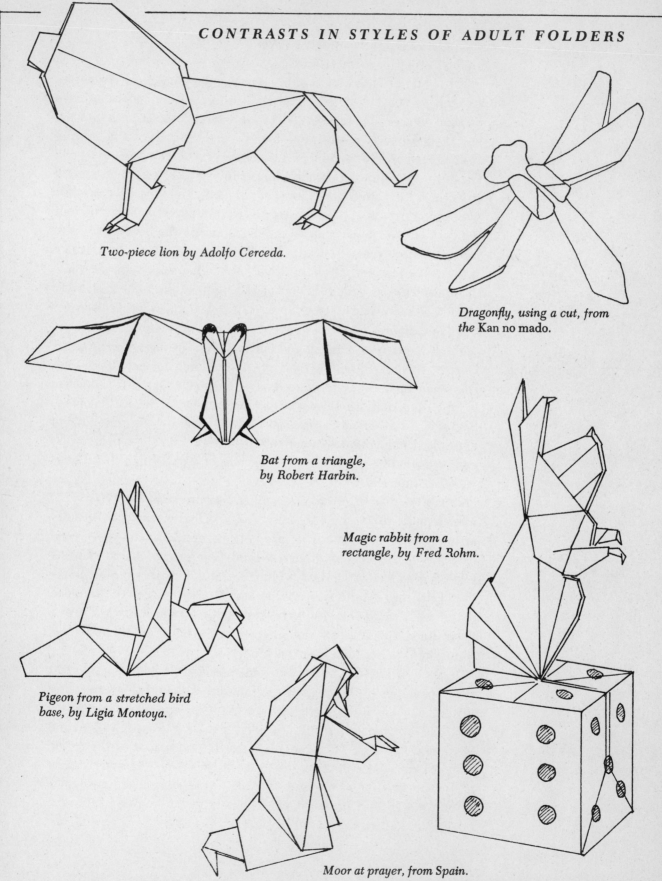

*Two-piece lion by Adolfo Cerceda.*

*Dragonfly, using a cut, from the Kan no mado.*

*Bat from a triangle, by Robert Harbin.*

*Magic rabbit from a rectangle, by Fred Rohm.*

*Pigeon from a stretched bird base, by Ligia Montoya.*

*Moor at prayer, from Spain.*

lines. On page 14 is shown her pigeon, which can be contrasted with the Moor at prayer, of Spanish origin. Another dimension in which figures vary is their three-dimensional quality. Boxes, furniture, flowers and boats are frequently folded as three-dimensional objects. Human and animal figures, however, are generally folded as flat two-dimensional figures, as illustrated by the figures on page 14.

## MODERN ORIGAMI

This book, which I titled *Modern Origami*, contains instructions for folding about fifty of my own creations, of which there are about one hundred in all at this writing. I have maintained the restriction of folding from a square piece of paper without cutting or pasting, and have developed a style in the direction of systematic, stylized, artistic and three-dimensional forms. One reason for not cutting— which is frequently used to achieve realistic details such as ears, legs, etc.—is that it destroys the beauty of the straight line. It also prevents the search for more complex bases and techniques of folding. It is frequently the restriction of the uncut paper which provides the stylized effect, which adds to the beauty of the folded figure.

In order to make artistic creations without cuts and still make long and thin limbs, I have found it necessary to shift from commercially available origami paper to aluminum-foil paper. This paper is truly modern and happens to be ideal for paper folding. The paper on one side makes folding or refolding possible, while the aluminum foil helps to hold the creases in place. Aluminum-foil paper is available in the United States in large quantity at Christmas time as gift-wrapping paper. It is usually packaged in rolls of varying lengths, usually 26 inches wide. I have used two sizes of paper extensively: 8½ inches square when the roll is cut in thirds and 6¼ inches when cut in fourths. Except for extremely intricate objects such as the crab, objects generally can be folded readily with 6¼-inch-square foil paper, provided it is thin. Finely embossed paper is generally easier to fold than papers with smooth finishes or heavy embossing.

Aluminum-foil paper also comes in a variety of colors and has a luminous surface which is ideal for displaying your origami. Patterns and even words on the paper sometimes provide impressive effects when used with the appropriate figures. For example, a brand of paper called India Foil features stripes of different colors. A paper with two or three stripes of bright colors makes an attractive insect. The problem in using foil paper is that it is necessary to accumulate a collection of the suitable weight and design at Christmas time and cut it to the desired size when needed. Directions for cutting rolls of paper are given in Chapter II. Packages of aluminum-foil paper should be available in bookstores and in larger quantities from the J. C. Campbell Paper Company, 30 Freight Street, Pawtucket, Rhode Island.

To make larger objects, sheets two to three feet square can be used, but there is need for corresponding increase in strength. Heavy aluminum foil backed with kraft paper can be used for medium-size objects. It is used to cover doors and is available at Christmas time. Thin cardboard with aluminum foil bonded on both sides is also commercially available at art-supply stores. I have seen it used as background for an aquarium.

One should always be on the lookout for newer material. Recently I discovered Forbon, which comes in sheets 30 by 50 inches, is as stiff as cardboard, but can be folded and unfolded and still hold its creases. The heavier form of Forbon seemed to be too heavy to fold. However, I followed my son's suggestion of wetting the material, and discovered that it became flexible like leather when wet and then hardened into a rigid form as it dried. The best procedure probably is to wet one side only, retaining flexibility on one side for ease of folding and rigidity on the other to hold creases. By taping two lightweight sheets together and using the wetting process, I have been able to make a standing stork 42 inches tall, which stands on its own two feet without any aid. Forbon is manufactured by NVF Company, Parsons Paper Division, Wilmington, Delaware.

## HOW INNOVATION BEGAN

My interest in paper folding stems from a background of Japanese culture mixed with American influence. My parents were immigrants from Japan to the United States, and I was brought up in the Japanese community in and around Los Angeles. I was sent to a Japanese-language school after public school was over and on Sundays to a Buddhist church Sunday school. My background was therefore steeped in Japanese culture maintained by the transplanted immigrants, and, among other things like judo, and go, I learned some origami, probably from my mother. I can remember folding the inside-out boat, the crane, the trick boat, the helmet, the *yakkosan* and the ball (water bomb). Beyond childhood, however, I showed little interest in origami until after my son, William, was born. By this time, 1952, I was at the University of Connecticut teaching psychology, and I found the chairman of the department, Professor

Weston Bousfield, folding traditional figures from available books. His father was a medical missionary in China, and he derived his interest in origami from that. I bought a few books myself and began to relearn some of the traditional figures. Much of the activity was concentrated at Christmas time, when it was possible to decorate the Christmas tree with balls and the sitting crane. I remember making mobiles for some of my neighbors. At one point I concentrated on airplanes and boats for my son. My first innovation was a modification of the inside out boat, on which I managed to add a sail and a keel. Another was a swept-back-wing airplane and a Mosquito bomber. The latter I later modified to make my prize-winning entry for the *Scientific American* First International Paper Airplane Contest in 1967. I also modified the traditional charcoal brazier to make an attractive four-point star.

The beginning of active creation came in 1955 when I showed my sister-in-law, Mrs. George Sakoda, in California the four-pointed star. She thought it would be nice if it could be changed into an eight-pointed star. I thought about it overnight, and came up with a maneuver—sinking the center point—which would allow me to make eight equal-length points rather than four long ones with four stubby ones in between. Thus the eight-point star was born. The development which followed was almost automatic. I found that when I pulled apart the eight-point star and refolded it along existing creases, I could easily make a number of animals with little effort. In rapid succession I made Pegasus, the angelfish, a camel, a seal, a kitten. Others evolved more slowly, and some involved development of a unique move. An example is the T-fold, from which it was possible to make the giraffe, the donkey and the peacock. In a sense what I did was make many creases when folding the eight-point star, and follow the creases to make stylized and attractive figures.

## ANATOMY OF THE EIGHT-POINT STAR

By analyzing the eight-point star it is possible to understand to some extent why it has been the basis of many attractive figures. The process of sinking the point produces four additional points and permits folding the inside of the paper. This lends variety over the simpler bird base, which has tended to be overworked. The eight-point star is also three-dimensional in form, and many of the figures made from it preserve this quality. On page 19 is shown the creases of an eight-point star, which form an interesting pattern. It can be readily seen that there are many creases scattered throughout the paper. By following these, rather than making arbitrary folds, it is possible to obtain a stylized effect. Furthermore, many of these lines make a kite form, which is the basis of the bird base and has an attractive proportion. The proportion of the width of the kite form at its widest point to its length is $1:\sqrt{1/2}$ or $1:1.707$. The proportions of the golden section, sometimes considered to be ideal proportions, are $1:1.618$. This is the proportion of two lines when the shorter length is to the longer as the longer is to the sum of the two.

My usual approach was not to try to make some definite object, although I did attempt this on occasion with some success, but rather to fold the paper along established creases until a familiar form appeared. When this happened I attempted to improve upon it, but with an eye to preserving the beauty of the object rather than providing realistic details. Sometimes the improvement was made over a period of several years and would arise when I tried to make an object and found that I had forgotten how to make it. The emphasis on beauty came partially from reactions from friends who admired certain of the figures more than others. My first creation which I considered artistic was the giraffe, with its emphasis upon the long, slender neck.

## MORE INNOVATIONS

Other innovations followed the eight-point star. Here again the main effort was to attempt a different combination of folds—i.e., to find a new base rather than to fold a predetermined figure. Part of the paper was turned inside out after folding the eight-point star, and this enabled me to fold the penguin and the bishop. I stumbled upon the stretched bird base, from which I was able to make the standing crane, the praying mantis and the tin soldier. The blintz fold, which I learned from Randlett's book, when combined with the bird base produced a base with eight points, which I used for the elephant and the bear, among others. The offsetting of the center of the bird base produced flaps of three different lengths, providing a variation in proportions. The combination of the blintz fold and the use of an offset center led to the insects with staggered legs. I narrowed the frog base to make human figures and the ape, a move which was facilitated by use of thin aluminum-foil paper. The frog base applied to a blintz fold provided a basis for the sixteen-point chrysanthemum.

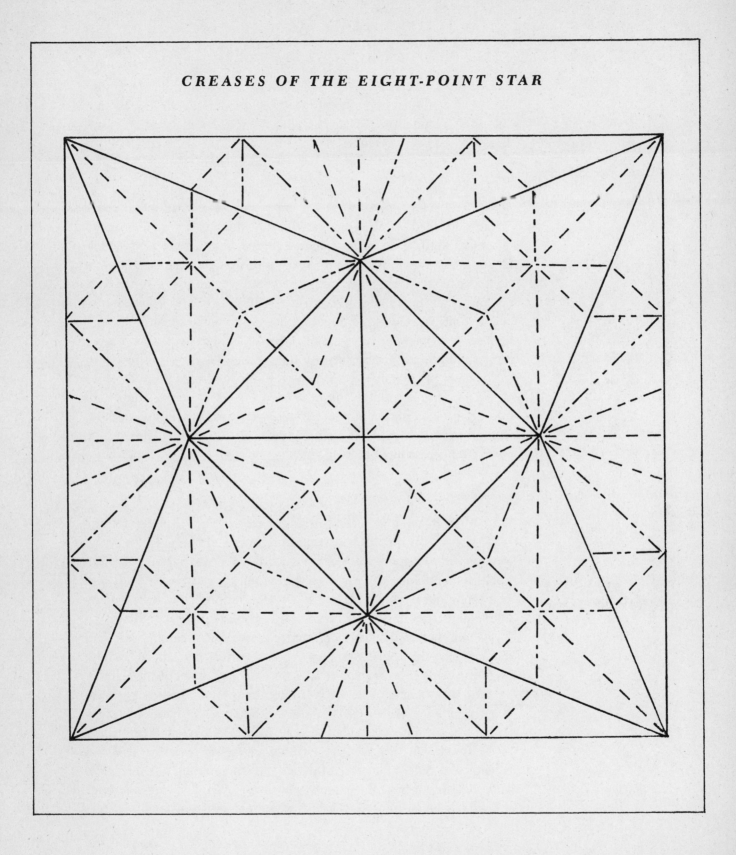

CREASES OF THE EIGHT-POINT STAR

The most complex fold has been the crab, which is based on double-blintzed fold combined with an offset-center bird base. My most recent innovation has been a coolie-hat figure made from a frog base. Only the earlier and simpler of the folds are included in this volume, but they include some of my favorites—the owl, the standing crane, the nun, the praying mantis and the mask.

## ORIGAMI PINS

One of the unfortunate features of paper is its lack of rigidity. Sooner or later a folded figure is mutilated out of shape. I have made many efforts to find means of making the folded figure more permanent. Coating the paper with plastic spray increases its rigidity to only a limited extent. I have tried painting melted wax on boats, but it does not make the boat sufficiently rigid. In 1965 I read in a newspaper article that paper was hardened with resin to make furniture, and I immediately went to the garage to try out polyester boat resin on some foldings, and to my surprise they turned very hard. This led to the origami pin, which was made by folding figures from small pieces of aluminum-foil paper (usually four inches square), and then soldering a bar pin to a wire. It made the origami figure durable enough to wear. Polyester resin, however, is brittle, and the legs of insects tend to break off.

## ORIGAMI FOR WHOM?

"Modern origami," then, refers to creative adult paper folding of a type which emphasizes stylized figures and the use of colorful aluminum-foil paper, while staying within the restrictions of traditional paper folding. It involves the search for new basic folds and new techniques. It is hoped that the modern approach will spur many adults and older children to take up the hobby of paper folding.

From personal experience and observation I can recommend modern origami to the following types of people particularly. Those planning trips to outer space will find origami not only a suitable pastime for cramped quarters but also a means of converting sheets of paper into useful objects. I also recommend origami to fellow computer programmers who already have practice in fitting parts into a functioning whole. Those who want to quit smoking will find it helpful to pull out a piece of paper and start folding whenever the smoking urge arises. Executives who must attend boring meetings will find origami useful as a means of amusing themselves. Travelers will find that paper folding, which requires only a supply of paper, is a good way to become acquainted with children, fellow passengers and airline hostesses. Parents with children who have nothing to take to school for "Show and Tell" would do well to learn origami and teach their children a few simple figures. Teachers who want to win the respect of boys should learn to fold airplanes which fly and boats which sail. The teaching of origami provides an excellent opportunity to combine Oriental art, exercise in finger dexterity and discipline in following written directions. It is an ideal pastime for invalids. For the blind and the near-blind, it should be a challenge to learn to fold.

The novice is warned, however, that following directions for folding paper may not be as simple as he thinks. The next chapter should be studied carefully, for it gives the basic vocabulary and instructions for following folding directions.

# CHAPTER II

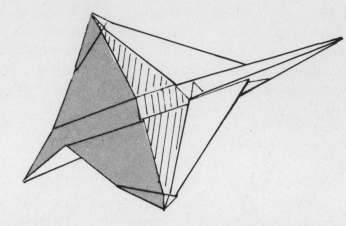

# Basic Moves

**M**any people have told me that they or their children started to learn origami from a beginner's book, but had to give up because they simply could not follow the written directions. Many books, it must be admitted, contain poor instructions. Even well-written directions, however, are not always easy to follow. Symbols and terms used to describe moves have to be learned, but these are not always uniform from book to book. Fortunately, a set of symbols and terms have evolved from the published work of Yoshizawa, Randlett, Harbin and others, and most of them are followed in this book. Some of the terms, such as "blintz fold" and "water bomb," may not sound very Oriental, but language has a way of growing somewhat illogically. It is important for the novice to learn these terms and symbols used in the instructions and drawings before tackling figures beyond this chapter. The best procedure is to follow each lesson step by step, folding the figure as directed.

**BASIC SYMBOLS**

The most important symbols to learn are those for the valley and mountain folds. Valley folds are folded inward and are indicated by dashes (— — — —). Mountain folds are folded outward and are shown by a series of dots and dashes (— · · — · · —). Following directions is impossible unless this distinction is learned very early. There are also symbols for turning a figure over and for tucking in or opening a portion of the figure.

**FOLLOWING DIRECTIONS**

For each of the original figures there is a photograph at the beginning of the chapter. Examine this carefully before starting to fold. In the directions there will be references to wings, nose, etc., and it is helpful to know what these terms refer to. The photographs are also helpful in seeing the overall appearance of the finished product, which is difficult to show in a line drawing.

Directions are given at each point in at least three different ways, and it is important to give close attention to all of them. Using just a portion of them is apt to allow the folder to jump to the wrong conclusion.

*First*, read the written instruction. The words "valley fold" written out may be more explicit for some than seeing a set of dash lines. Written directions can convey instructions which cannot be put down in a drawing. For example, one can easily say, "Repeat Steps 3–5 on the reverse side," but this cannot be easily conveyed in the form of a drawing.

*Second*, look at the accompanying drawing. In this book, the written instruction and the drawing for it are placed next to each other to make the association of the two easier. The uncolored underside of the paper is shown by a solid gray shade. Cross-hatchings have been added to the drawn figures to show the different layers of paper, and to emphasize a particular portion being folded. In the drawing moves are indicated in two different ways: by means of dash or dot-dash lines, which show the location and the direction of the folds to be made, and, less exactly, by means of an arrow, indicating where one of the points begins and ends. Folding toward the back is shown by partially hidden arrows.

*Third*, examine the next drawing, *ignoring the broken lines and arrows*. It shows the appearance of the figure after the required folds have been made. Origami instructions are programmed so that after each step a check is possible. If the two do not agree, obviously an error has been made. (An error in the drawing is possible, but not as likely as an error by the folder.)

Only after the first step has been completed successfully should one go on to the next step—i.e., read the directions for the second step. It is surprising the number of times a person jumps from Step 1 to Step 3 without even checking to see that Step 1 is done correctly.

Redundancy in information can be valuable in assuring communication. Even with some redundancy it is not feasible to convey the details of every step explicitly. For one thing, there is a limit to the number of drawings one can use. Some of the details must be left to the imagination and ingenuity of the folder. Whenever difficulty is encountered in doing a particular step, one must learn to persevere. An error has been made, and it is necessary to find it. One should recheck all of the directions first—the written, the broken lines, the arrows, the next drawing—to see if he has fully understood all of them. You may need to go back and review some basic step. An analytical approach is highly desirable. One might mumble such things as "This must be the leading edge of the plane, since it has disappeared. To make it disappear was it a valley or mountain fold that was used?" It helps to explain the difficulty to someone else, since in so doing one reviews the instructions more carefully. "Look at this stupid instruction—it's impossible. It says here that— Oh, oh, I think I get it now; never mind, never mind, I can do it."

The worst kind of perseverance is repeating the same move over and over again. It may be expedient to experiment a little, since this may produce the desired result. In so doing you may end up with a different but attractive invention of your own. Unless you are patient, you are apt to give up the entire enterprise in disgust. If the paper you are working with becomes wrinkled or you lose your place, it is time to get a drink of water and start over again. If necessary, one can set the project aside and come back to it again. Although instructions are written to be as explicit as possible, complete and foolproof instructions are impossible, and it is desirable for learners to view problems as challenges, which, when conquered, make success all the sweeter.

Some writers of origami instruction prefer to put as much of their instruction as possible into the diagrams, and they relegate written instructions to a secondary role. They are then likely to miss some important uses of verbal instructions. One is that they can be read aloud by someone, generally an adult, while the folder, frequently a child, looks at the diagram and attempts to fold a figure; it is then possible for a teacher or a parent, for example, to aid in teaching origami without even knowing how to fold. A second use for the written instruction is in teaching a group by explaining verbally the steps which are to be taken. It is not sufficient simply to say, "Do this"; more explicit instructions, such as "Fold sides to the center line," which frequently can be taken directly from the written directions, are desirable.

## FOLDING

A flat surface, such as a table top or a large book, is desirable in making folds. When one is folding on a flat surface a mountain fold is generally made by turning the figure over and making a valley fold in the same location. When both a valley and a mountain fold are to be made the valley fold should be made first, turning over the side of the figure on which the mountain fold is required. A second valley fold can then be made immediately without turning the figure over. Some folders learn to fold while holding the paper in their hands, but the use of a flat surface is recommended initially.

The novice tends not to make neat, sharp creases. Whenever a fold is indicated, it is generally advisable to make a sharp crease, with one's finger or fingernail, even if the fold then has to be opened part way again. This not only makes a straight line, but also helps to take wrinkles out of the rest of the paper. Excessive handling of the paper should be avoided when making a finished model, since it robs the paper of clean and crisp appearance. It takes practice to make some of the intricate folds; the novice should not be discouraged if at first his finished product does not have the crisp appearance of the one in the photograph.

It is sometimes helpful to make preliminary creases, particularly when two or more folds need to be made at the same time. These preliminary creases insure that the folds are made along the lines indicated on the diagram. For difficult steps it is also helpful initially to make all of the preliminary creases so that the valley and mountain folds are all made in the right direction. The folds will then fall into position of their own accord. This technique can be used on, for example, the foot fold, which is one of the more difficult folds to make. With increased experience, many of the preliminary folds become unnecessary. Some experienced folders take considerable pains not to use preliminary folds which leave unnecessary crease marks on the paper.

**BASIC LESSONS**

This chapter begins with two lessons in learning the symbols. The learner should go through each of these lessons step by step, following the instructions. To avoid confusion, initially the result of a step is given in a separate diagram; later the result is combined in the same diagram with the instruction for the next step. These two lessons are followed by practice on the picture frame, the blintz fold and the kite form. There is a lesson on the accordion fold, which is a relatively new term for a valley fold followed by a mountain fold. Kasahara refers to it as *dan-ori,* or step fold. This is followed by instructions for folding the SST (supersonic transport) origami airplane, which won the origami design award in the First International Paper Air-

## THE SST ORIGAMI AIRPLANE

plane Contest in 1967. It made aviation history in the *1968 World Topics Year Book,* and is also included in *The Great International Paper Airplane Book.* Step 3, which calls for "tucking in of the leading edge of wings under the nose of the plane," tends to cause difficulty. When this happens, close scrutiny of the broken lines will show that half of the lines are dot-dash (mountain fold) lines and the other half dash (valley fold) lines. The arrow indicates that the fold is to fit under the nose (the nose is the one with the point, of course).

The lessons on reverse and accordion folds are important. They are used to put a bend into a folded section. The reversal turns the folded portion inside out, which may not always be desirable. The inside reverse fold places the bent portion inside the fold, while in the outside reverse fold it goes on the outside. There are two accordion folds—the foot fold and the crimp fold. The foot fold, which is also called a double inside reverse fold, manages to avoid the reversal of the paper and is the one I generally use to put bends in legs and arms. Preliminary creases can be made to guide the folding, but these are not always necessary, particularly when the limb to be folded is very narrow. Instead of using two reverse folds, I have preferred to use the instruction calling for a valley fold, followed by pushing up the center line from below. The crimp fold also puts a bend in a fold section without reversal of the paper. The difference between the foot fold and the crimp fold is that in the foot fold the bend is made toward the folded edge and in the crimp fold toward the open end. A practice lesson on the reverse and accordion folds is included.

These lessons are followed by instructions for cutting a single square sheet and also for cutting square sheets from a roll. Folding a box from an 8½-by-11 sheet of paper will provide good practice in carrying out the instructions. This is followed by instructions for the modified Chinese junk, which can be skipped if found to be too difficult.

The more thoroughly the lessons in this chapter are learned, the better will be the chances of succeeding in later chapters.

## SYMBOLS TO LEARN

a. *Read instruction.*
b. *Note symbols in diagram.*
c. *Carry out instruction.*
d. *Check your result.*

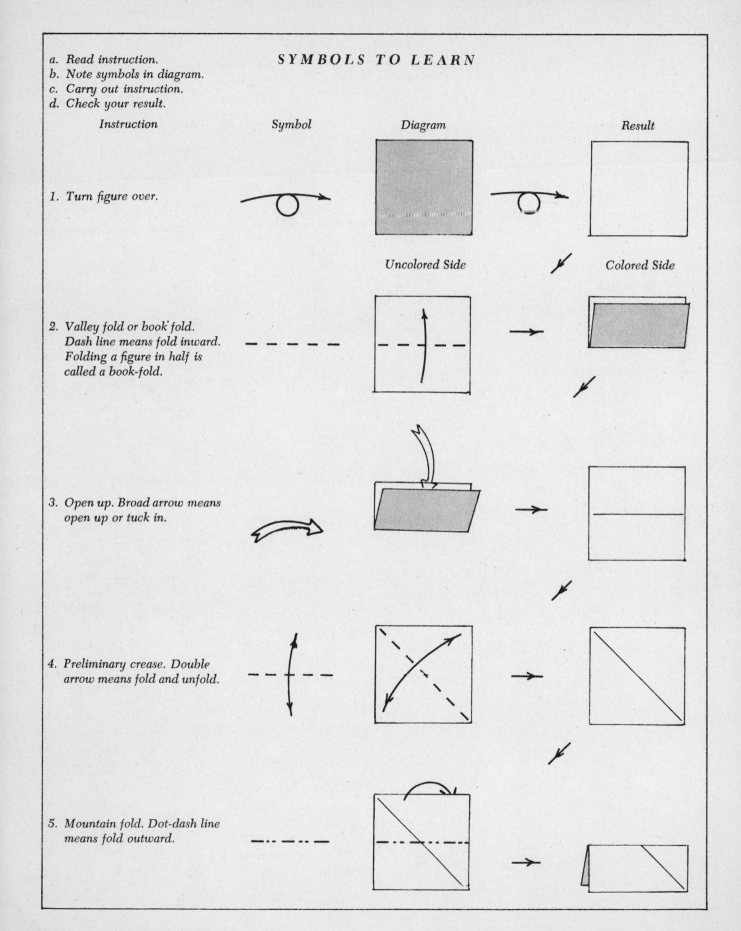

| Instruction | Symbol | Diagram | Result |
|---|---|---|---|

1. Turn figure over.

Uncolored Side     Colored Side

2. Valley fold or book-fold. Dash line means fold inward. Folding a figure in half is called a book-fold.

3. Open up. Broad arrow means open up or tuck in.

4. Preliminary crease. Double arrow means fold and unfold.

5. Mountain fold. Dot-dash line means fold outward.

# PRACTICE ON SYMBOLS

*Written instructions have been omitted. Carry out each instruction in turn.*

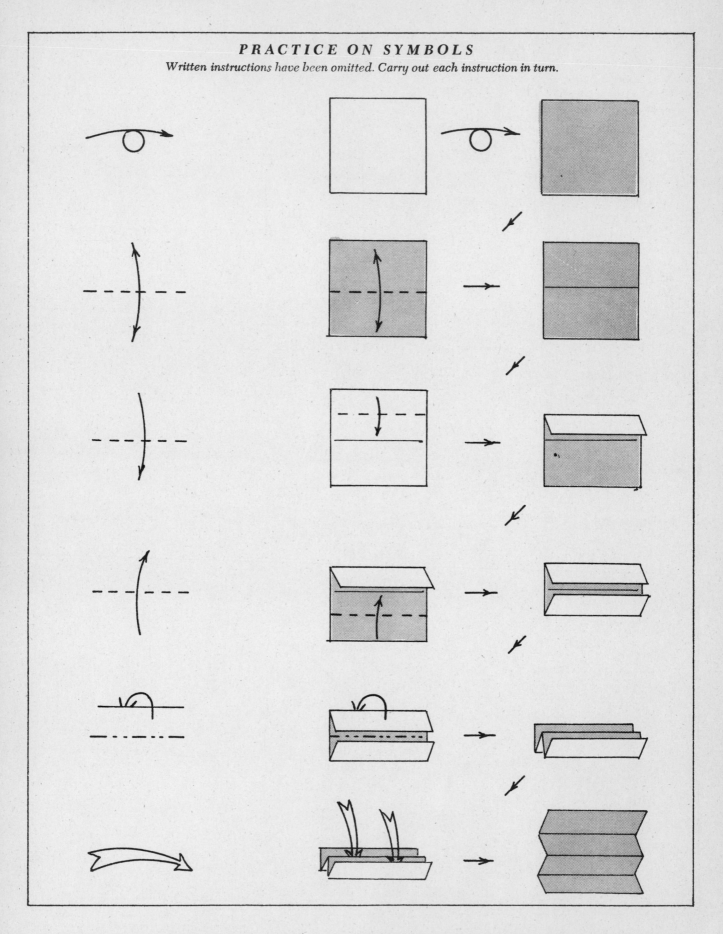

# THE PICTURE FRAME

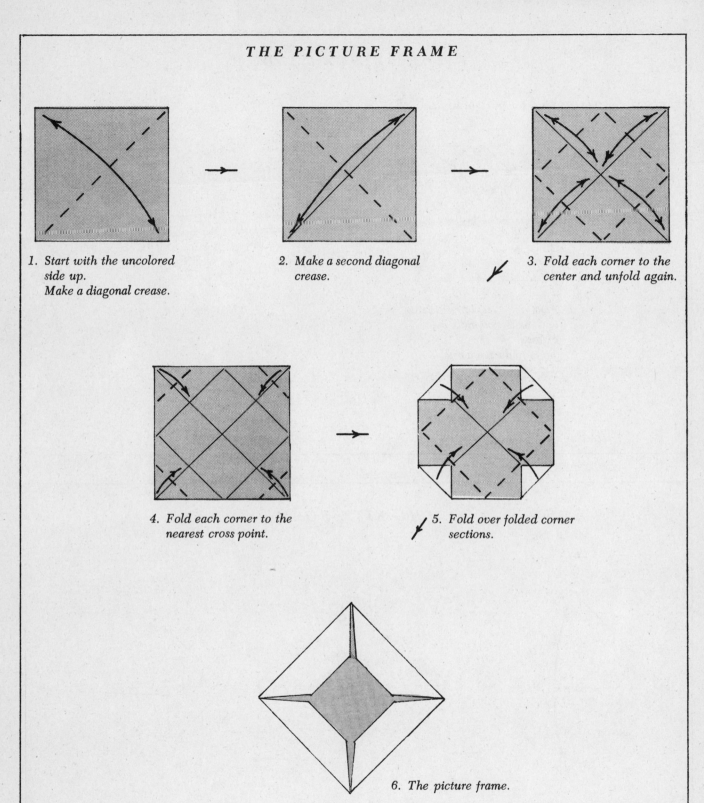

1. Start with the uncolored side up.
   Make a diagonal crease.

2. Make a second diagonal crease.

3. Fold each corner to the center and unfold again.

4. Fold each corner to the nearest cross point.

5. Fold over folded corner sections.

6. The picture frame.

Valley fold _ _ _ _ _ _            Mountain fold _ _ .. _ _ .. _

# THE BLINTZ FOLD

*This provides a square with eight corners.*

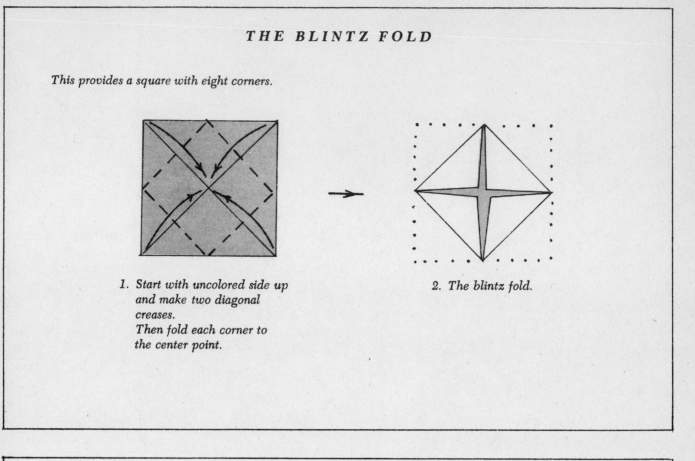

1. Start with uncolored side up and make two diagonal creases.
   Then fold each corner to the center point.

2. The blintz fold.

# THE KITE FORM

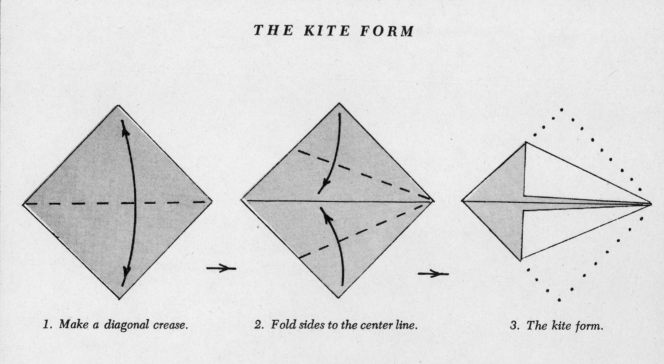

1. Make a diagonal crease.

2. Fold sides to the center line.

3. The kite form.

# THE ACCORDION FOLD

*Made of the alternating mountain and valley folds.
Three different uses are shown here.*

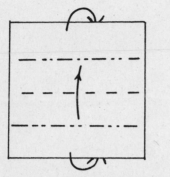

**A1.** *Valley-fold the square in half.
Then mountain-fold each
part in half again.*

**A2.** *Accordion-folded square.*

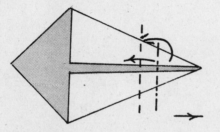 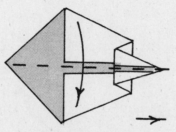

**B1.** *Start with a kite form.
Valley-fold the point and
follow it with mountain fold.*

**B2.** *Book-fold the accordion-
folded figure in half.*

**B3.** *Accordion-folded point.*

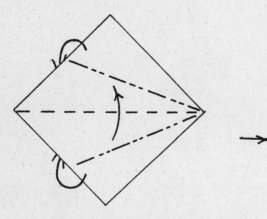

**C1.** *Make a diagonal valley fold.
Then mountain-fold both
sides to center line.*

**C2.** *Converging accordion fold.*

# THE SST ORIGAMI AIRPLANE
## WINNER OF THE ORIGAMI AWARD IN THE FIRST
## INTERNATIONAL PAPER AIRPLANE
## CONTEST, 1967

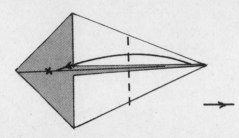

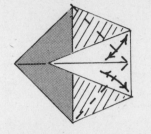

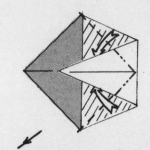

1. *Make a kite form, using bond paper 8½ inches square. Fold the nose back to the point marked x.*

2. *Make a preliminary crease on the leading edge of wings by folding and unfolding.*

3. *Tuck in leading edge of wings under the nose of the plane.*

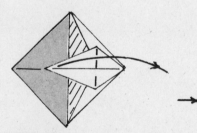

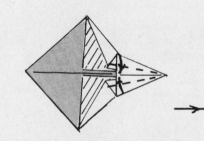

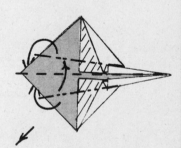

4. *Fold down nose at its widest point.*

5. *Narrow down nose by folding edges to center line.*

6. *Accordion-fold. Fold plane lengthwise inward in half. Then fold down wings, following the angle of the nose.*

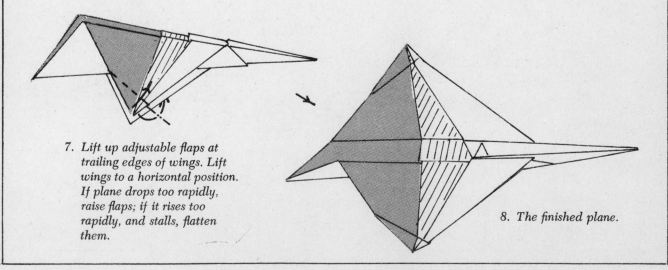

7. *Lift up adjustable flaps at trailing edges of wings. Lift wings to a horizontal position. If plane drops too rapidly, raise flaps; if it rises too rapidly, and stalls, flatten them.*

8. *The finished plane.*

# THE INSIDE REVERSE FOLD

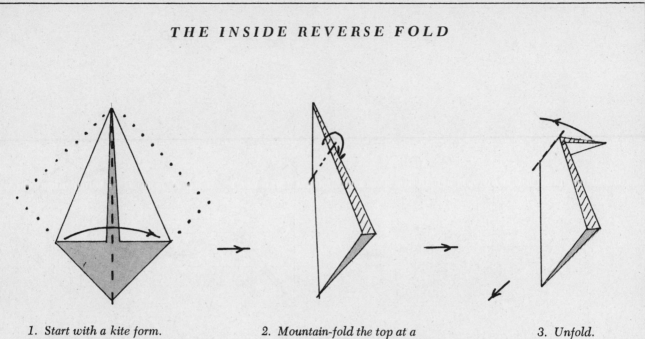

1. *Start with a kite form.*
   *Book-fold the figure in half.*

2. *Mountain-fold the top at a*
   *desired angle in the direction*
   *of the open edges.*

3. *Unfold.*

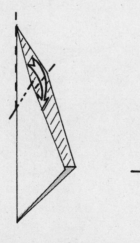

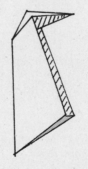

4. *Open figure partially and*
   *bend point down between*
   *flaps, using old creases. (It is*
   *necessary to reverse the*
   *vertical fold from a mountain*
   *to a valley fold.)*

5. *The inside reverse fold.*

*Valley Fold* — — — — —          *Mountain Fold* — — · — — · — — ·

# THE OUTSIDE REVERSE FOLD

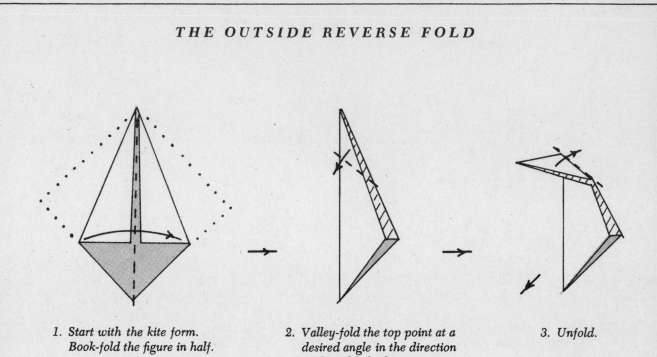

1. *Start with the kite form. Book-fold the figure in half.*

2. *Valley-fold the top point at a desired angle in the direction of the folded edge.*

3. *Unfold.*

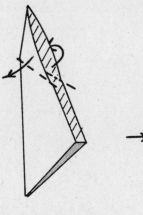

4. *Open figure wide and bend point down outside the two flaps and along creases. (It is necessary to reverse the vertical fold from a mountain to a valley fold.)*

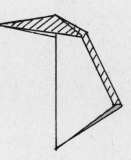

5. *The outside reverse fold.*

Valley fold  — — — — —

Mountain fold  — — -- — -- —

# THE CRIMP FOLD

A bend toward the open edge which avoids reversal of the folded edge. It is indicated by an accordion fold converging toward the folded edge.

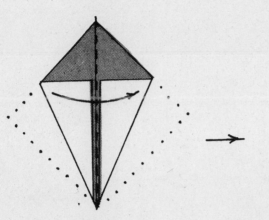

1. *Start with the kite form. Book-fold the figure.*

2. *Preliminary accordion fold. Valley-fold down and mountain-fold up to position in desired direction.*

3. *Unfold.*

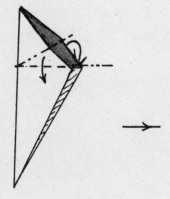

4. *Open out flap and accordion-fold both sides downward.*

5. *The crimp fold.*

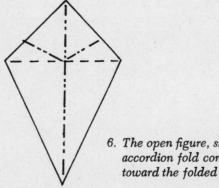

6. *The open figure, showing the accordion fold converging toward the folded edge.*

# THE FOOT FOLD

A bend toward the folded edge which avoids reversal of the folded edge. It can also be seen as a double inside reverse fold—one reverse fold followed by another. It is indicated by an accordion fold converging toward the open end.

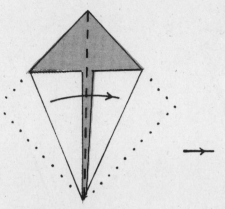

*1. Start with a kite form. Book-fold the figure.*

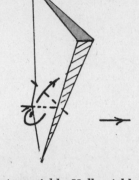

*2. Preliminary folds: Valley-fold up and mountain-fold down and position point in the desired direction toward the folded edge.*

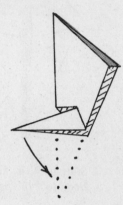

*3. Unfold.*

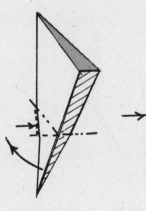

*4. Open up figure and valley-fold point in desired direction.*

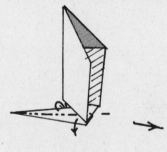

*5. Mountain-fold bend point by pushing up center line from below.*

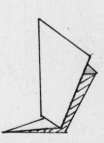

*6. The foot-fold bend.*

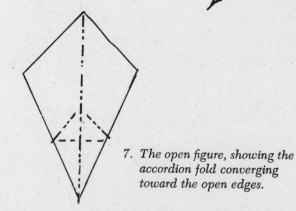

*7. The open figure, showing the accordion fold converging toward the open edges.*

## PRACTICE ON REVERSE FOLDS

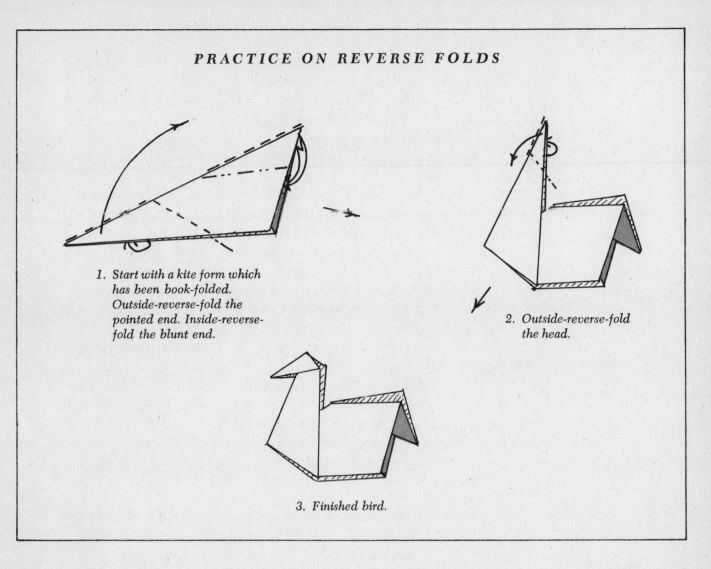

1. Start with a kite form which has been book-folded. Outside-reverse-fold the pointed end. Inside-reverse-fold the blunt end.

2. Outside-reverse-fold the head.

3. Finished bird.

## PRACTICE ON ACCORDION FOLDS

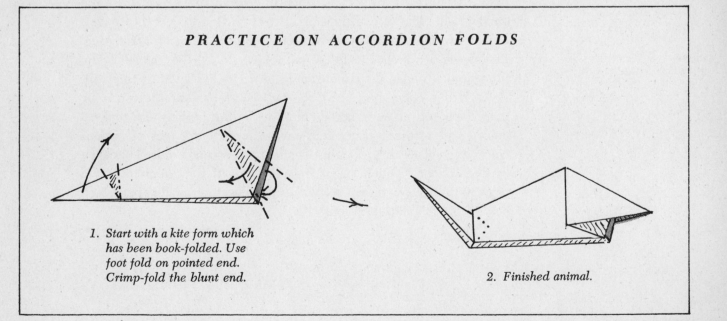

1. Start with a kite form which has been book-folded. Use foot fold on pointed end. Crimp-fold the blunt end.

2. Finished animal.

## HOW TO CUT A SQUARE

Occasionally one finds an irregular piece of paper which needs to be cut into a square. This is an easy task if there is at least one right-angle corner, since two diagonal folds will quickly make a square. On page 39 are shown directions for cutting a single square sheet from an irregular piece of paper, using a pair of scissors.

Cutting paper from a roll is a bit more complicated. A roll of foil paper is usually 26 inches wide and varies in length from a short piece about 30 inches long to such lengths as 5, 10, 15, 25 feet or more. The shorter pieces are usually found in boxes of four to six rolls of assorted colors, while the longer ones are sold in individual rolls. The assortments provide variety in color—a desirable feature for paper folders. The longer lengths are easier to handle.

The width of the paper to some extent determines the size of the sheets to be cut, if wastage of paper is to be avoided. If the paper is 26 inches wide, it can be cut in fourths to produce sheets 6¼ inches along one dimension, leaving an inch for trimming; if a larger size is desired for intricate figures or to make a larger model, the paper can be cut in thirds to produce sheets 8½ inches along one dimension; if an even larger size is desired, it can be cut in half to produce sheets 12 inches wide. If the paper happens to be 30 inches wide, a similar principle can be used to produce sheets 7 or 9½ inches wide.

The aim in cutting paper is not only to cut sheets of the desired dimensions, but also to cut a reasonable number each time so that the job can be done efficiently. For this purpose a paper cutter a little larger than the size of the sheet being produced is desirable. A 12-inch paper cutter is a suitable size for most origami work. The paper cutter can be used to cut twelve or more sheets at one time, but in order to do this it is necessary to fold the roll of paper properly. The detailed illustrated directions for cutting paper from a roll are given on page 40. The roll of paper is first accordion-folded into panels twice as wide as the sheets to be produced, plus an inch for trimming. For sheets 6¼ inches wide the panels should be 13½ inches wide; for 8½-inch paper the panel should be 18 inches wide. If there are several rolls containing short sheets, about three of these can be placed on top of one another prior to folding panels. To make a package of assorted paper it is necessary to cut paper of various colors and collate them. Quantities of cut paper can be stored between cardboard cut ⅛ inch larger than the size of the paper and held tight with rubber bands. This is advisable because rolled paper which has been cut will tend to curl.

# HOW TO CUT A SQUARE

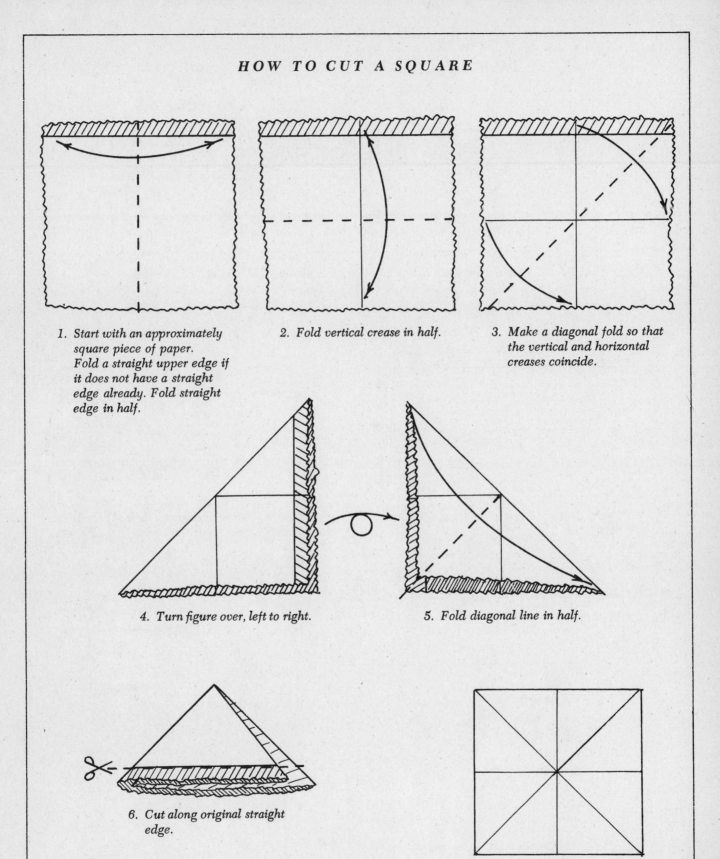

1. Start with an approximately square piece of paper. Fold a straight upper edge if it does not have a straight edge already. Fold straight edge in half.

2. Fold vertical crease in half.

3. Make a diagonal fold so that the vertical and horizontal creases coincide.

4. Turn figure over, left to right.

5. Fold diagonal line in half.

6. Cut along original straight edge.

7. A square.

# HOW TO CUT SQUARE SHEETS FROM A ROLL

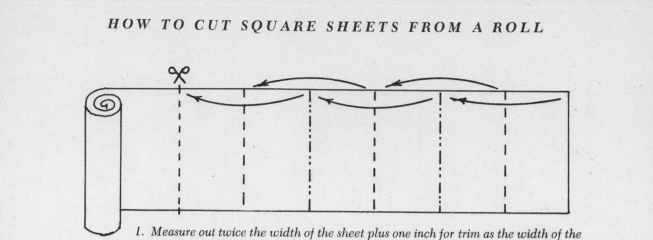

*1. Measure out twice the width of the sheet plus one inch for trim as the width of the first panel (e.g., 2 x 6¼″ + 1″ = 13½″). Valley-fold the first panel and follow this with alternate mountain and valley folds to fold about six panels. Cut off the panels.*

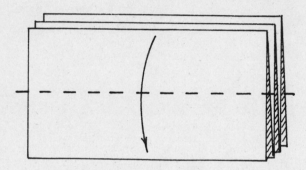

*2. Fold the panels lengthwise in half.*

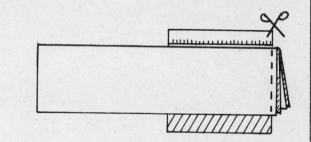

*3. Keeping the folded edge against the rule of the paper cutter, trim off uneven edges on the right. Turn panels over so that the trimmed edge is on the left.*

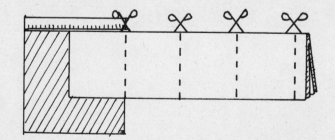

*4. Beginning with the trimmed edge, cut exact widths of sheets—e.g., four packets 6¼″ wide.*

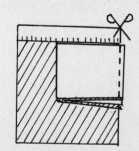

*5. Take each packet and trim the open untrimmed edges, leaving half of the trim for the folded edge. Turn the packet around carefully to trim the folded edge.*

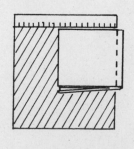

*6. Make certain that all sheets are aligned, and cut off the folded edge.*

## HOW TO FOLD A BOX

Knowledge of box folding is a necessity for a paper folder, particularly if he wants to impress an admirer who has been watching him fold. It is embarrassing to present half a dozen loose finished figures to a person when he has no way of holding them. They do not fit into a pocket or even a pocketbook, and would be easily crushed if they were so stored. A box folded of paper, on the other hand, is impressive because it fills a need miraculously. Paper place mats, maps, folders, concert programs, meeting handouts are all fair game for the folder in need of material for a box. Paper $8\frac{1}{2}$ by 11 inches is a suitable size, and directions for folding a box from a sheet that size are given on page 42. The box is adapted from Marie Gilbert Martin's "weaver's shuttle" box. Even with the same-size paper it is possible to vary the size of the box by varying the width of the sides. By narrowing the widths the box can be made shallower and bigger. The box can be shortened by increasing the size of the turned-over edge. The turned-over edge can be made to reach the bottom of the box by making one set of margins twice that of the other. The box is then neater and sturdier. The neatness can be increased by making a diagonal mountain fold on the loose corners on two sides of the box. This is the form in which Marie Gilbert Martin explained the construction of her box. If the paper is square, a box can be constructed simply by choosing two sets of margins, one wider than the other, rather than by folding to the center line. By making two boxes, one slightly bigger than the other, it is possible to make a box with a cover. The advantage of this type of box is not only its flexibility, but also the neatness of its mode of construction and its final appearance. An excellent ashtray can be made by folding a box from an IBM card.

# HOW TO FOLD A BOX

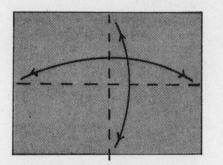

1. Start with a rectangular sheet (8½ x 11 sheets are suitable). Make preliminary creases for vertical and horizontal center lines.

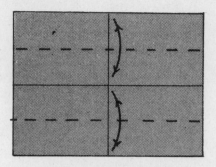

2. Fold narrow sides to the center line and unfold.

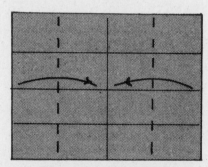

3. Fold wide sides to the center line. (If a square sheet is used, fold the first folded sides narrower than the second.)

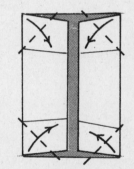

4. Diagonal-fold corners by valley-folding folded edge to crease lines.

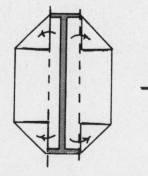

5. Fold raw edges over folded corners.

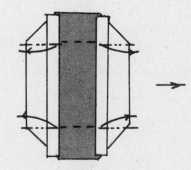

6. Open up sides of box and reverse folds as shown.

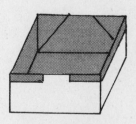

7. Finished box.

THE
MODIFIED
CHINESE
JUNK

The last instruction in this chapter is for a modified Chinese junk. The stern is that of a Chinese junk, modified to produce a rudder. The bow is that of an inside-out boat, modified to produce a sail. The combination produces a boat capable of catching the wind in its sail and taking off. It is undoubtedly too difficult for the novice, and he should return to it after a little more experience in folding. It is placed in this chapter because the Chinese junk is a modification of a box.

There are a number of new moves required in folding the modified Chinese junk, which contribute to the difficulty of completing it. In Step 7 there is a compound fold which involves folding the sides and the end simultaneously. The folding of the sides must be followed through with a fold of the end. In Step 11 folding the upper edge of the boat to the lower edge requires that a triangle be formed at the end. Seen from the inside of the boat this fold is a rabbit-ear fold. In Step 12 the sides of the boat at the bow are flipped inside out to lock the boat into place. This is a clever move which is also a unique one. At Step 13, pulling out a folded portion to form a deck is a seldom-used move that is undoubtedly one of the cleverest moves known in traditional origami.

*THE MODIFIED CHINESE JUNK*

# THE MODIFIED CHINESE JUNK

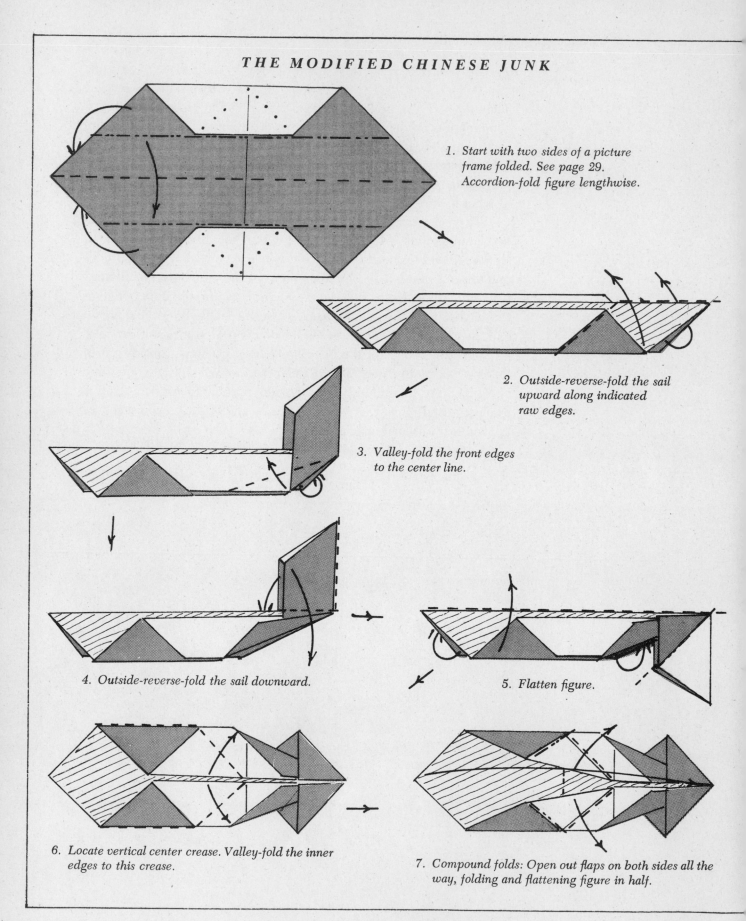

1. Start with two sides of a picture frame folded. See page 29. Accordion-fold figure lengthwise.

2. Outside-reverse-fold the sail upward along indicated raw edges.

3. Valley-fold the front edges to the center line.

4. Outside-reverse-fold the sail downward.

5. Flatten figure.

6. Locate vertical center crease. Valley-fold the inner edges to this crease.

7. Compound folds: Open out flaps on both sides all the way, folding and flattening figure in half.

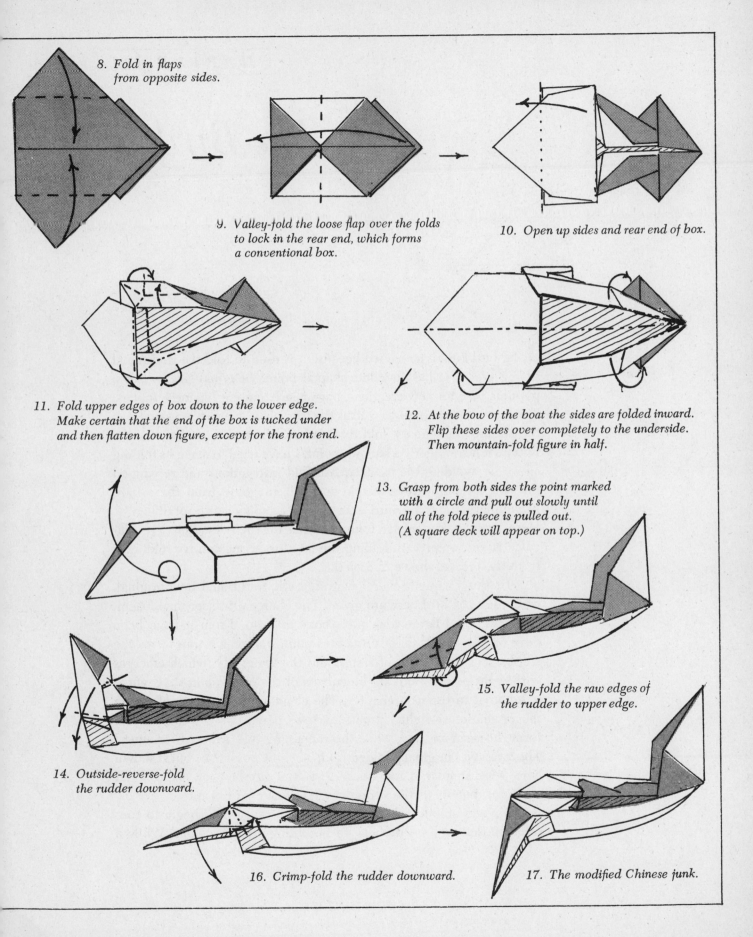

8. *Fold in flaps from opposite sides.*

9. *Valley-fold the loose flap over the folds to lock in the rear end, which forms a conventional box.*

10. *Open up sides and rear end of box.*

11. *Fold upper edges of box down to the lower edge. Make certain that the end of the box is tucked under and then flatten down figure, except for the front end.*

12. *At the bow of the boat the sides are folded inward. Flip these sides over completely to the underside. Then mountain-fold figure in half.*

13. *Grasp from both sides the point marked with a circle and pull out slowly until all of the fold piece is pulled out. (A square deck will appear on top.)*

14. *Outside-reverse-fold the rudder downward.*

15. *Valley-fold the raw edges of the rudder to upper edge.*

16. *Crimp-fold the rudder downward.*

17. *The modified Chinese junk.*

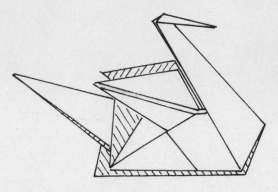

# CHAPTER III

# The Bird Base

The bird base is so named because it is used to fold the traditional sitting crane. It has four kite-shaped points of equal size and is a popular base for new creations, particularly among Japanese folders. To get to the bird base, as well as the frog base, it is necessary to learn the square preliminary fold first. While it is a simple step, for the initiate it is frequently a hangup point. I have tried to make its folding easier by avoiding the usual squash-fold instructions and relying on the simpler inside reverse fold instead. In going from the square preliminary fold to the bird base there is a similar source of difficulty. Here again inside reverse folds are used for their simplicity. If difficulty is encountered in folding the bird base, one can try folding it from the creases shown in Step 6.

In this chapter several figures, both traditional and original, which use the bird base are given. The charcoal brazier, or hibachi, is a traditional figure and quite boxy in form. From it have been developed two innovations: the four-point star, which transforms the stubby legs into points of a star, and the water lily, which emerges with eight points. Both are precursors of the eight-point star, which is featured in the next chapter. The elegant sitting crane, of which the Japanese are rightly proud, narrows down two of the points to form the head and tail, while the remaining two are used for wings. The swan was originally folded from an eight-point star, but is shown here with simpler instructions. It is the simplest of my original creations, but rivals the sitting crane in grace and beauty.

Anyone able to fold the crane and the swan will begin to consider himself well on the way to becoming a paper folder. While a small child would be happy to be able to fold a picture frame, an adult can show off his first sitting crane or swan. Many people who approach origami as something childish, and therefore easy, drop out before they reach this point. Careful reading of the instructions, close examination of the drawings, and perseverance are necessary to fold the two birds, and once this lesson is learned it is easier to go on to more difficult figures. The modified Chinese junk might be tried at this point.

*THE SITTING CRANE*

# THE SQUARE PRELIMINARY FOLD

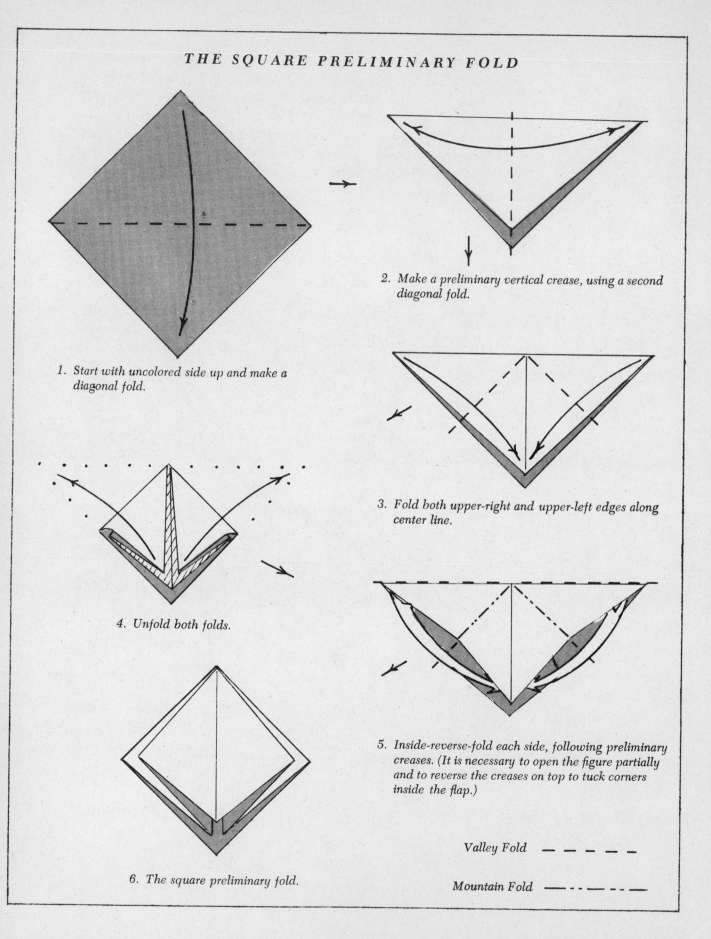

1. Start with uncolored side up and make a diagonal fold.

2. Make a preliminary vertical crease, using a second diagonal fold.

3. Fold both upper-right and upper-left edges along center line.

4. Unfold both folds.

5. Inside-reverse-fold each side, following preliminary creases. (It is necessary to open the figure partially and to reverse the creases on top to tuck corners inside the flap.)

6. The square preliminary fold.

Valley Fold — — — — —

Mountain Fold — — · — · — · —

# THE BIRD BASE

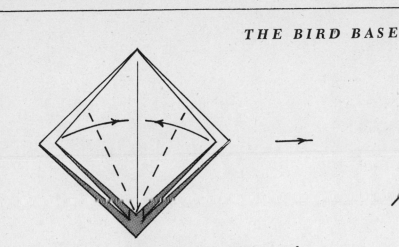

1. Start with a square preliminary fold. Fold lower sides of right and left flaps to center lines.

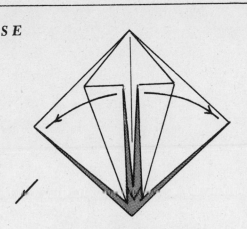

2. Unfold both right and left flaps.

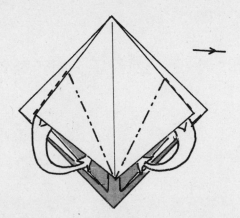

3. Use an inside reverse fold to tuck corners of left and right flaps inside. (It is necessary to reverse the creases on top and lift up the top sheet to slip in the side corner.)

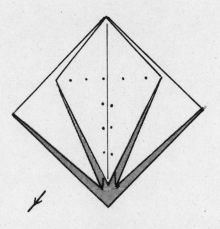

4. Repeat Steps 1–3 on reverse side.

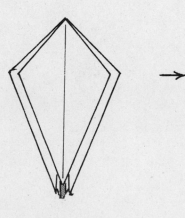

5. The bird base.

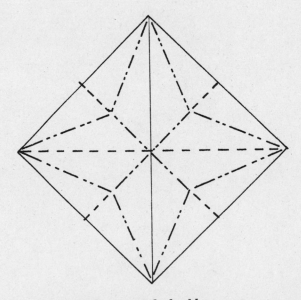

6. Creases of the bird base.

THE WATER LILY

THE CHARCOAL BRAZIER

THE FOUR-POINT STAR

THE SWAN

# THE CHARCOAL BRAZIER
*Traditional Japanese folding.*

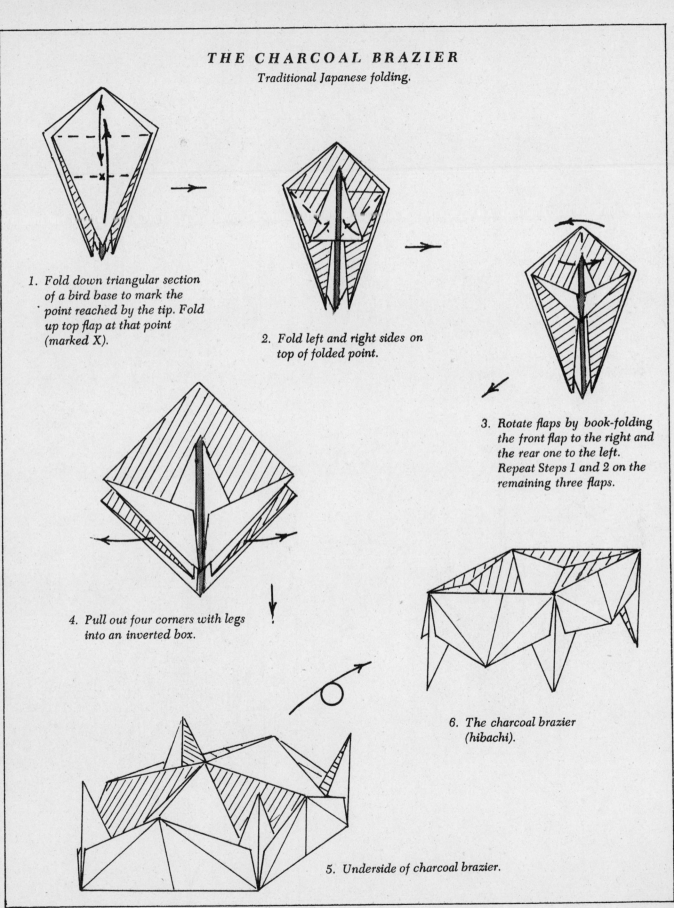

1. Fold down triangular section of a bird base to mark the point reached by the tip. Fold up top flap at that point (marked X).

2. Fold left and right sides on top of folded point.

3. Rotate flaps by book-folding the front flap to the right and the rear one to the left. Repeat Steps 1 and 2 on the remaining three flaps.

4. Pull out four corners with legs into an inverted box.

6. The charcoal brazier (hibachi).

5. Underside of charcoal brazier.

# THE FOUR-POINT STAR
Made from a modification of the charcoal brazier.

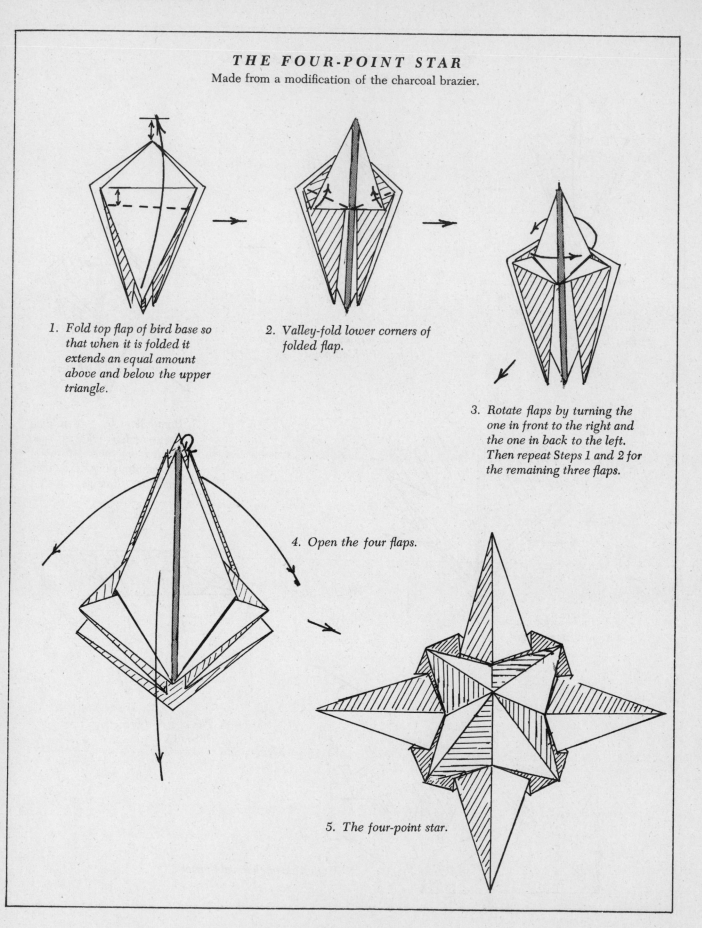

1. Fold top flap of bird base so that when it is folded it extends an equal amount above and below the upper triangle.

2. Valley-fold lower corners of folded flap.

3. Rotate flaps by turning the one in front to the right and the one in back to the left. Then repeat Steps 1 and 2 for the remaining three flaps.

4. Open the four flaps.

5. The four-point star.

# THE WATER LILY

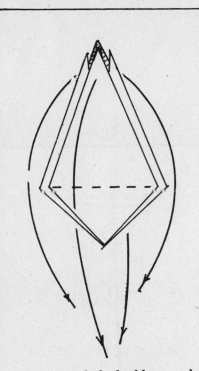

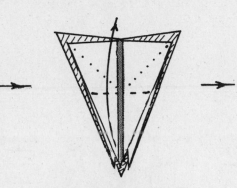

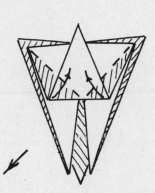

1. Start with the bird base, and fold each of the four flaps over the center point.

2. Valley-fold up the top flap. The fold is level with the hidden center point.

3. Fold in left and right corners of the folded flaps.

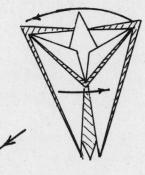

4. Rotate flaps by book-folding the front and rear flaps. Repeat Steps 2 and 3 on remaining three sides.

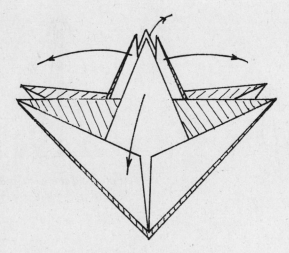

5. Open out the four points.

6. The water lily.

# THE SITTING CRANE
*Traditional Japanese folding.*

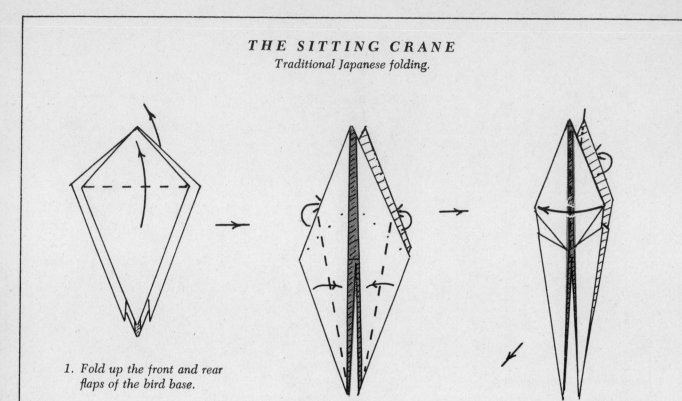

1. Fold up the front and rear flaps of the bird base.

2. Fold in lower sides to center line. Repeat behind.

3. Book-fold the figure front and back.

4. Fold up front flap as far as it will go. Repeat behind. (One becomes the neck, the other the tail.)

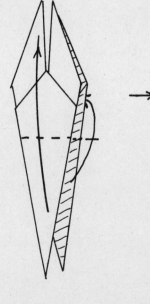

5. Book-fold the front and back, exposing the wider wings.

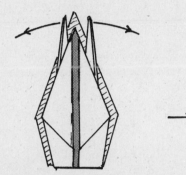

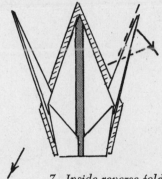

6. *Move neck and tail flush with edges of body.*

7. *Inside-reverse-fold one third of neck to form a head.*

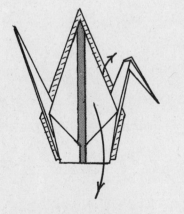

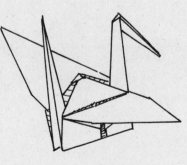

8. *Pull wings down into a horizontal position.*

9. *The sitting crane.*

## THE SWAN

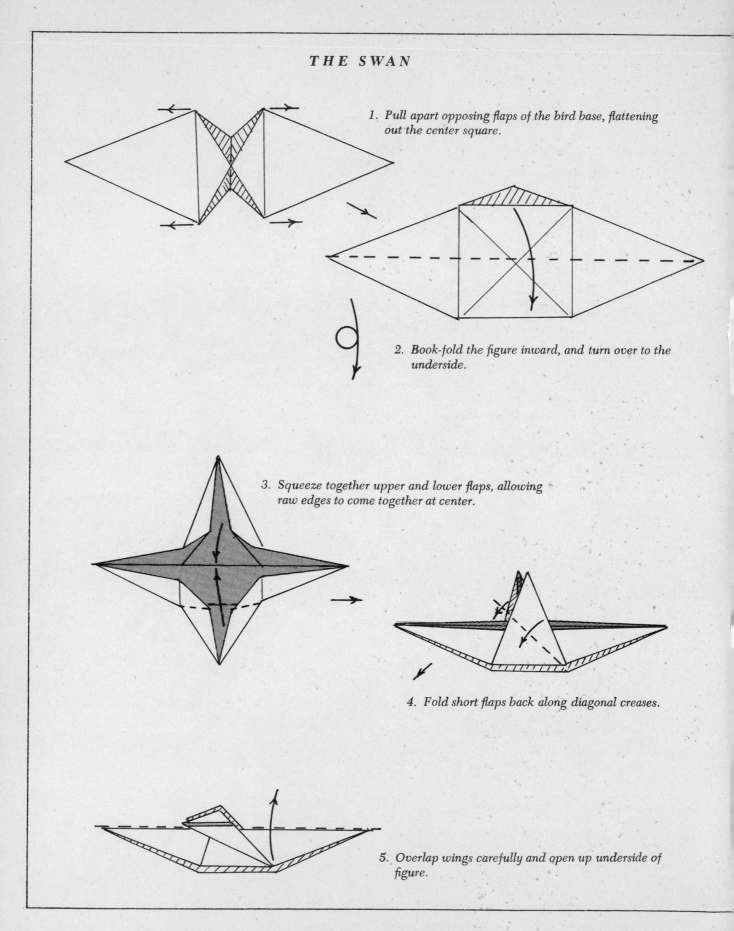

1. Pull apart opposing flaps of the bird base, flattening out the center square.

2. Book-fold the figure inward, and turn over to the underside.

3. Squeeze together upper and lower flaps, allowing raw edges to come together at center.

4. Fold short flaps back along diagonal creases.

5. Overlap wings carefully and open up underside of figure.

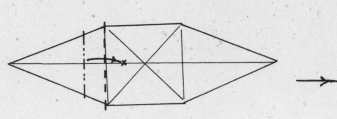

6. *Accordion-fold the tail.*

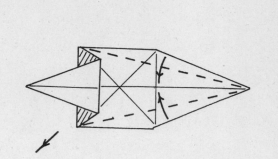

7. *Fold sides in from the corner of the square to the tip of the neck.*

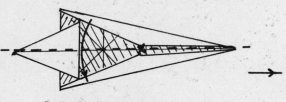

8. *Book-fold the figure.*

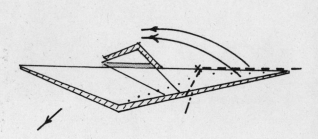

9. *Outside-reverse-fold the neck upward so that it almost touches the wings.*

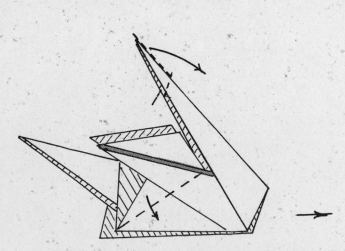

10. *Outside-reverse-fold the head. Open up the wings.*

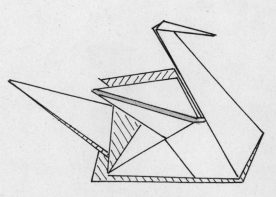

11. *The swan.*

*THE EIGHT-POINT STAR*

*THE SEAL*                    *PEGASUS*

# The Eight-Point Star

The eight-point star is the base for many of the figures shown in this book, and it is necessary to learn to make it well. The eight points provide for more complex models than is possible from the simple bird base. It also gives figures a definite three-dimensional quality, which is generally lacking in figures made from the bird base.

To go from the bird base to the eight-point star it is necessary to learn to sink the center point of the bird base. The folding of the eight-point star is then similar to that of the water lily, with one exception. This is the folding of the sides of the center square in Steps 6 and 7. Novices tend to make these folds too shallow, partly as a result of the tension on the paper caused by this move, which requires that the points of the center square be folded inward to make a three-dimensional form as the folding progresses.

Figures given in this chapter are relatively simple modifications of the eight-point star. These are the earliest inventions from this base, which relied upon making only a few modifications. Pegasus involves modifications only to sweep back two wings and to form a head. The remaining figures require that two opposing flaps be pulled out. This results in two long flaps at each end and two short side flaps, with convenient creases to guide the folding. In the seal the difficult step is to bring the head section perpendicular to the body, a form of T-fold, which is developed more fully in Chapter VI. A close examination of Figure 5 should help clarify the meaning of the instructions given for Figure 4.

The difficult step in the angelfish is the mouth; examination of the photograph may help here. The kitten has the first of many accordion folds used in this book. An accordion fold involves a series of valley and mountain folds. The first time, one can make preliminary creases as shown in the diagram prior to making the actual folds. The accordion fold of the tail of the kitten results in a change of direction **and** is the foot fold made from an open position. The face of the kitten is formed by accordion-folding along established creases. Here again a close look at the photograph will be helpful.

*THE KITTEN*

*THE ANGELFISH*

## SINKING THE POINT OF A BIRD BASE

Sinking the point results in the center point disappearing downward inside the figure.

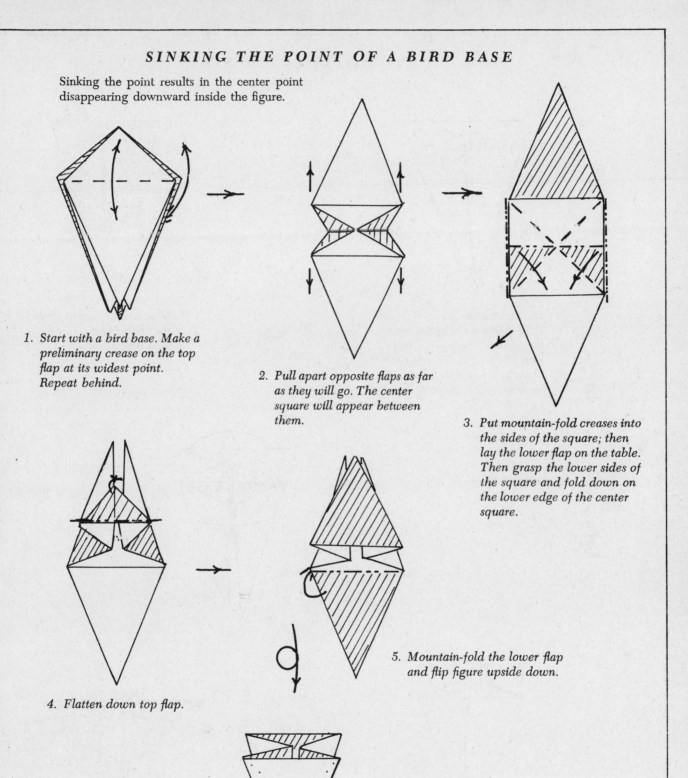

1. *Start with a bird base. Make a preliminary crease on the top flap at its widest point. Repeat behind.*

2. *Pull apart opposite flaps as far as they will go. The center square will appear between them.*

3. *Put mountain-fold creases into the sides of the square; then lay the lower flap on the table. Then grasp the lower sides of the square and fold down on the lower edge of the center square.*

4. *Flatten down top flap.*

5. *Mountain-fold the lower flap and flip figure upside down.*

6. *Sunken bird base.*

# THE EIGHT-POINT STAR

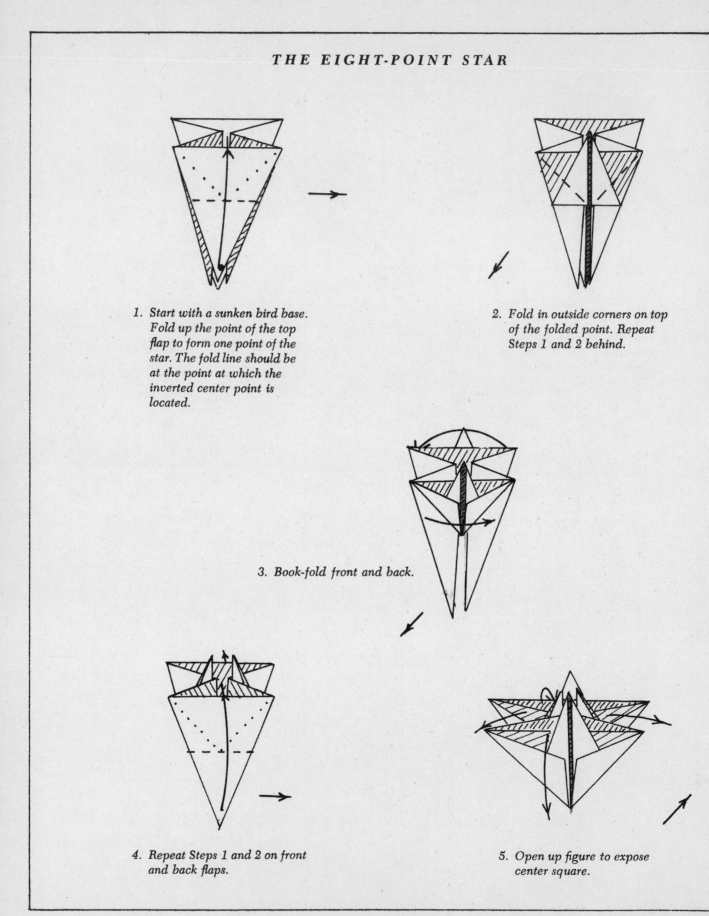

1. Start with a sunken bird base. Fold up the point of the top flap to form one point of the star. The fold line should be at the point at which the inverted center point is located.

2. Fold in outside corners on top of the folded point. Repeat Steps 1 and 2 behind.

3. Book-fold front and back.

4. Repeat Steps 1 and 2 on front and back flaps.

5. Open up figure to expose center square.

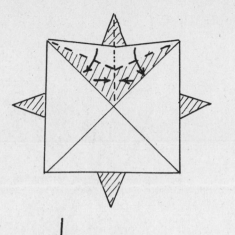

6. To make points on the center square, start with one side and fold the right half of it to the right diagonal line and the left half to the left diagonal line. At the same time squeeze the diagonal lines together. (Be sure that the edges fall along the diagonal lines.)

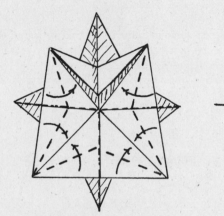

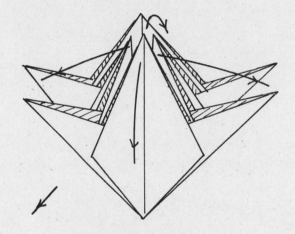

7. Repeat Step 6 on the remaining three sides. The figure becomes three-dimensional and difficult to fold.

8. Bring four points of the center square together, and sharpen all of the creases. Then unfold again.

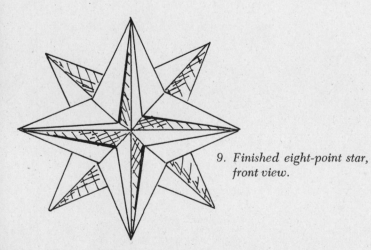

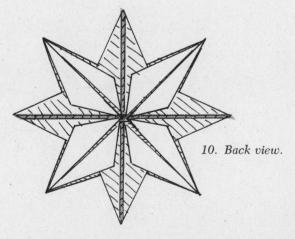

9. Finished eight-point star, front view.

10. Back view.

## PEGASUS

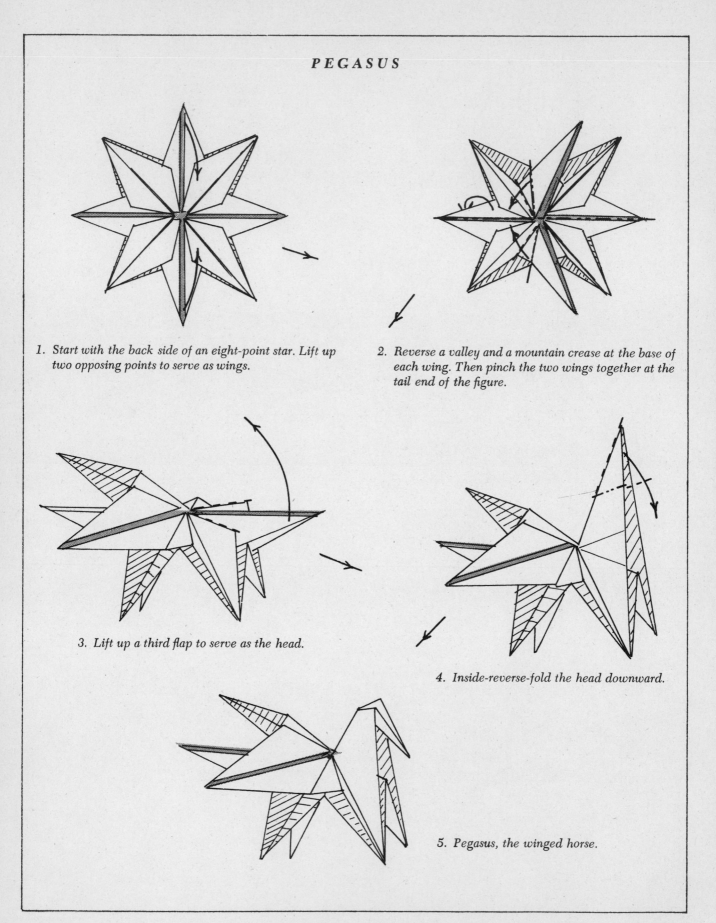

1. Start with the back side of an eight-point star. Lift up two opposing points to serve as wings.

2. Reverse a valley and a mountain crease at the base of each wing. Then pinch the two wings together at the tail end of the figure.

3. Lift up a third flap to serve as the head.

4. Inside-reverse-fold the head downward.

5. Pegasus, the winged horse.

# THE SEAL

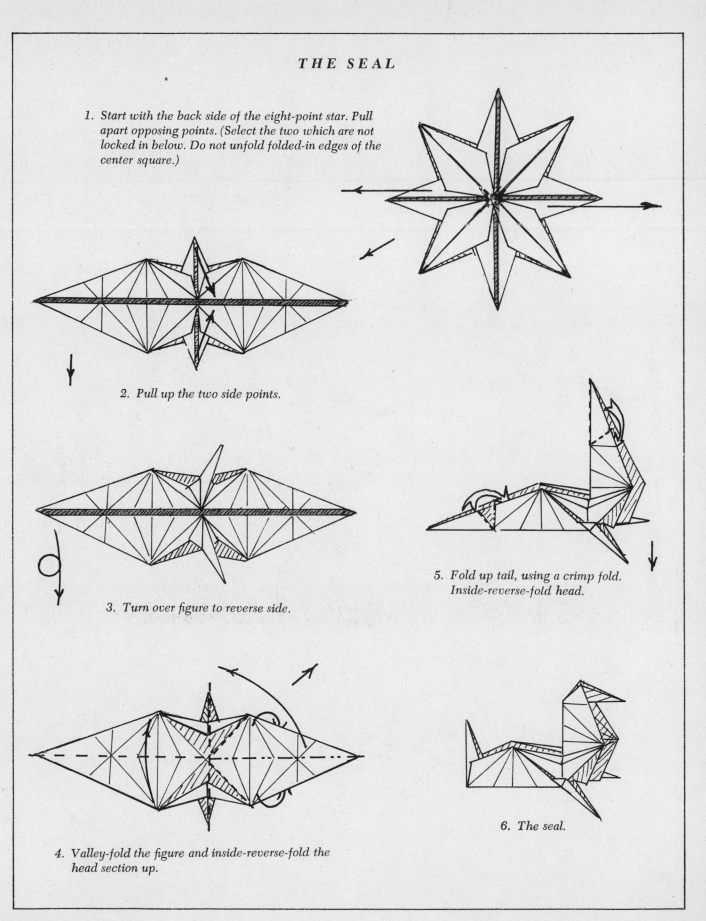

1. *Start with the back side of the eight-point star. Pull apart opposing points. (Select the two which are not locked in below. Do not unfold folded-in edges of the center square.)*

2. *Pull up the two side points.*

3. *Turn over figure to reverse side.*

4. *Valley-fold the figure and inside-reverse-fold the head section up.*

5. *Fold up tail, using a crimp fold. Inside-reverse-fold head.*

6. *The seal.*

# THE ANGELFISH

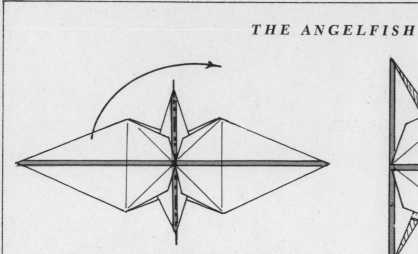

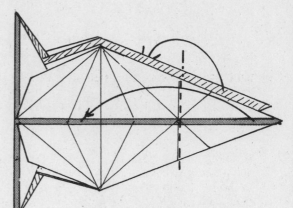

1. Start with an eight-point star with opposite points pulled apart. Mountain-fold the figure in half, bringing the two flaps together.

2. Valley-fold the point of the flap along existing vertical crease. Repeat behind.

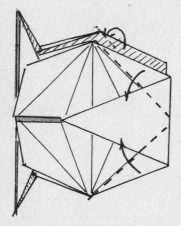

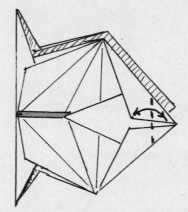

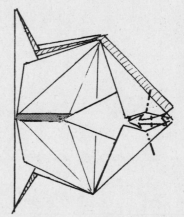

3. Valley-fold the upper and lower front corners. Repeat behind.

4. Make a preliminary crease for the mouth.

5. Open up the corner folds and tuck in the point of the upper flap.

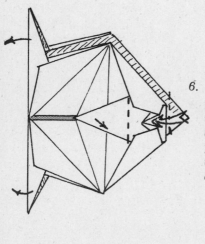

6. Finishing touches: Tuck the point of the flap on the underside into the mouth to hold front together. Open out fins. Pull back tails to give the figure a three-dimensional effect.

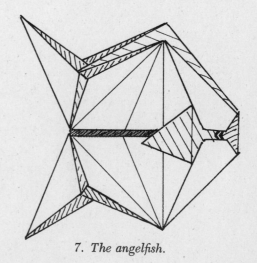

7. The angelfish.

## THE KITTEN

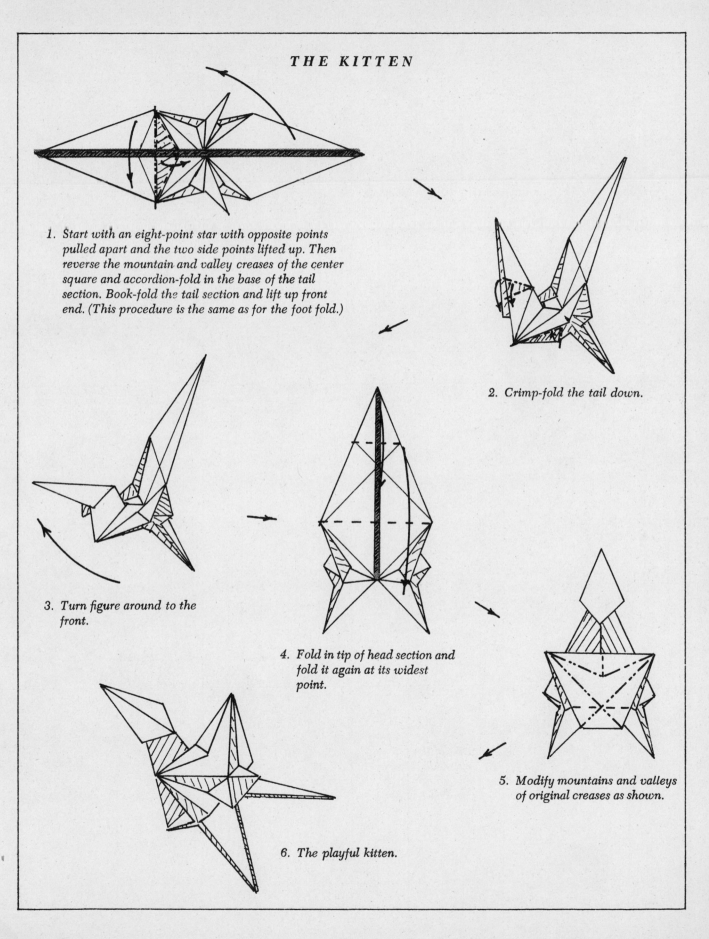

1. Start with an eight-point star with opposite points pulled apart and the two side points lifted up. Then reverse the mountain and valley creases of the center square and accordion-fold in the base of the tail section. Book-fold the tail section and lift up front end. (This procedure is the same as for the foot fold.)

2. Crimp-fold the tail down.

3. Turn figure around to the front.

4. Fold in tip of head section and fold it again at its widest point.

5. Modify mountains and valleys of original creases as shown.

6. The playful kitten.

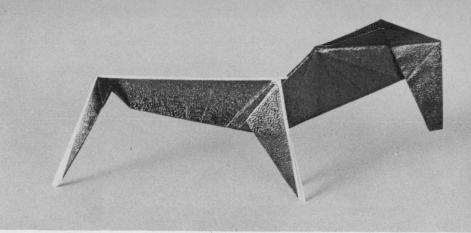

**THE HORSE**

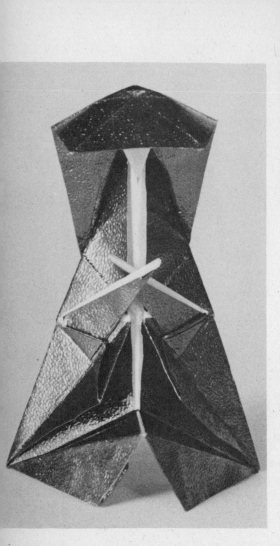

**THE NUN**

**THE COW**

**THE HIPPOPOTAMUS**

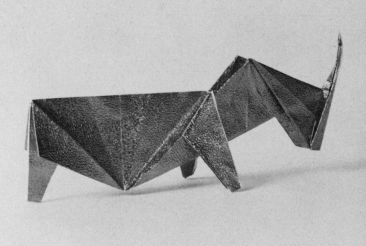

**THE RHINOCEROS**

# CHAPTER V

# Three-Legged Animals and the Nun

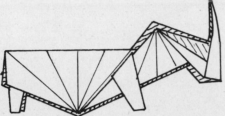

The three-legged animals—the horse, the rhinoceros, the hippopotamus and the cow—all start with the eight-point star pulled apart. The hind leg and the body are made of one long flap, the front legs from the short side flaps, and the neck and the head from the remaining long flap. In each animal a different feature is emphasized: the horse has its mane, the rhinoceros its horn, the hippopotamus its shovel-type mouth, and the cow its angular but elegant body. Few people are disturbed by the fact that the animals have only three legs.

The horse and the rhinoceros should offer little difficulty. The hippopotamus, which is a recent addition, involves a complex accordion-folded head section, which can be troublesome. Perseverance and experimentation may be necessary to achieve the desired effect. In folding the sides of the cow, the folds meet, not at the edge of the center square, but at the first crease beyond (see Figure 3).

The nun, which is the favorite of many, is included here because it was developed as a modification of the cow. The nun has a number of unique moves, including the face, which is turned inside out, the hood, which requires a flip from the back to the front, and a sitting posture. The beauty evident in the cow also appears in the nun, with the addition of a three-dimensional quality, a basic triangular form, and a praying posture which gives it a holy quality.

## THE HORSE

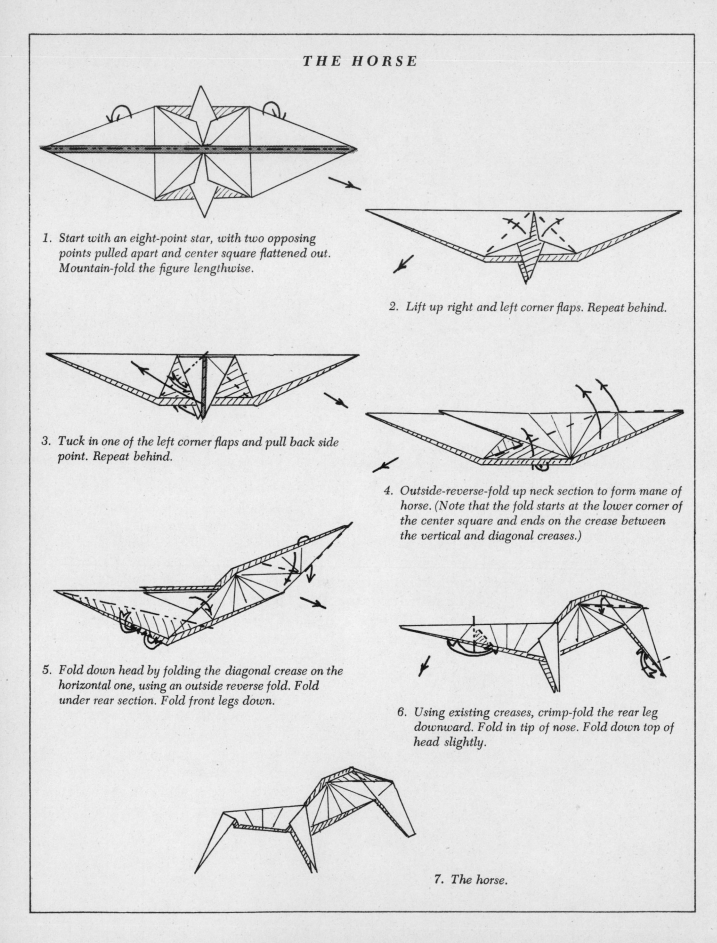

1. Start with an eight-point star, with two opposing points pulled apart and center square flattened out. Mountain-fold the figure lengthwise.

2. Lift up right and left corner flaps. Repeat behind.

3. Tuck in one of the left corner flaps and pull back side point. Repeat behind.

4. Outside-reverse-fold up neck section to form mane of horse. (Note that the fold starts at the lower corner of the center square and ends on the crease between the vertical and diagonal creases.)

5. Fold down head by folding the diagonal crease on the horizontal one, using an outside reverse fold. Fold under rear section. Fold front legs down.

6. Using existing creases, crimp-fold the rear leg downward. Fold in tip of nose. Fold down top of head slightly.

7. The horse.

## *THE RHINOCEROS*

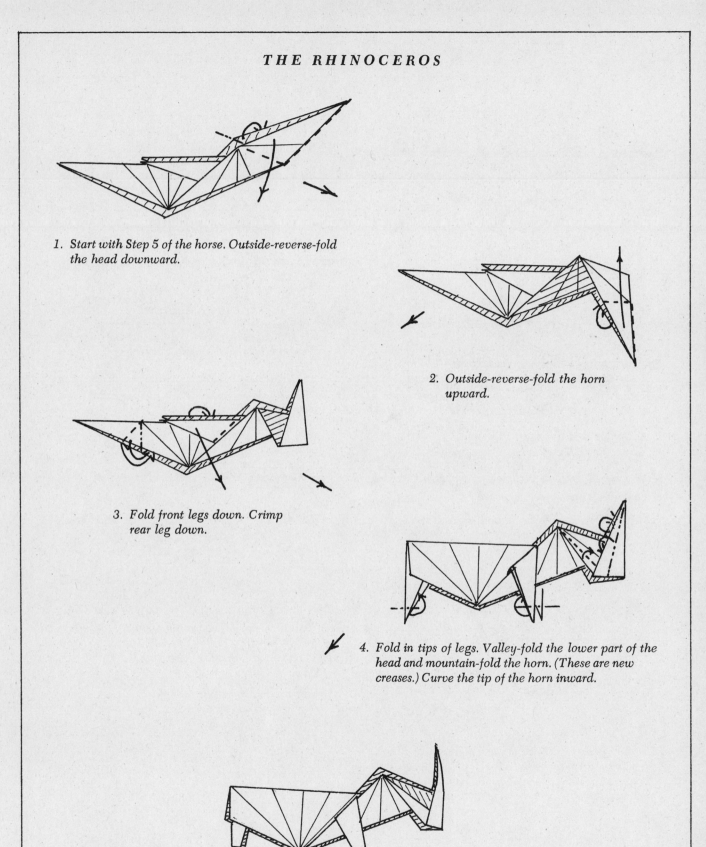

1. *Start with Step 5 of the horse. Outside-reverse-fold the head downward.*

2. *Outside-reverse-fold the horn upward.*

3. *Fold front legs down. Crimp rear leg down.*

4. *Fold in tips of legs. Valley-fold the lower part of the head and mountain-fold the horn. (These are new creases.) Curve the tip of the horn inward.*

5. *The rhinoceros.*

# THE HIPPOPOTAMUS

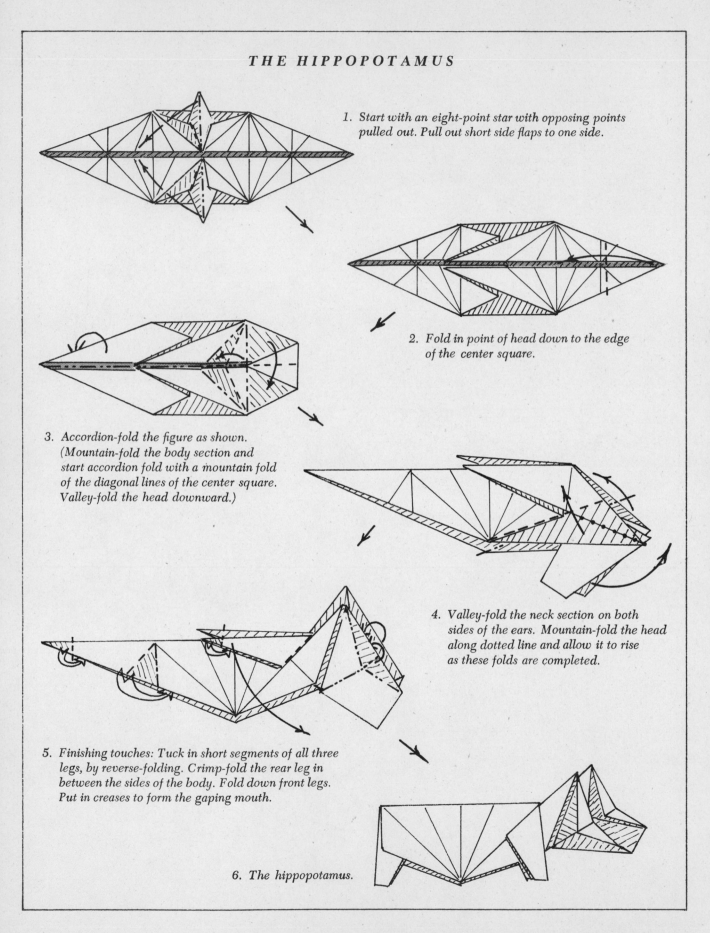

1. Start with an eight-point star with opposing points pulled out. Pull out short side flaps to one side.

2. Fold in point of head down to the edge of the center square.

3. Accordion-fold the figure as shown. (Mountain-fold the body section and start accordion fold with a mountain fold of the diagonal lines of the center square. Valley-fold the head downward.)

4. Valley-fold the neck section on both sides of the ears. Mountain-fold the head along dotted line and allow it to rise as these folds are completed.

5. Finishing touches: Tuck in short segments of all three legs, by reverse-folding. Crimp-fold the rear leg in between the sides of the body. Fold down front legs. Put in creases to form the gaping mouth.

6. The hippopotamus.

## THE COW

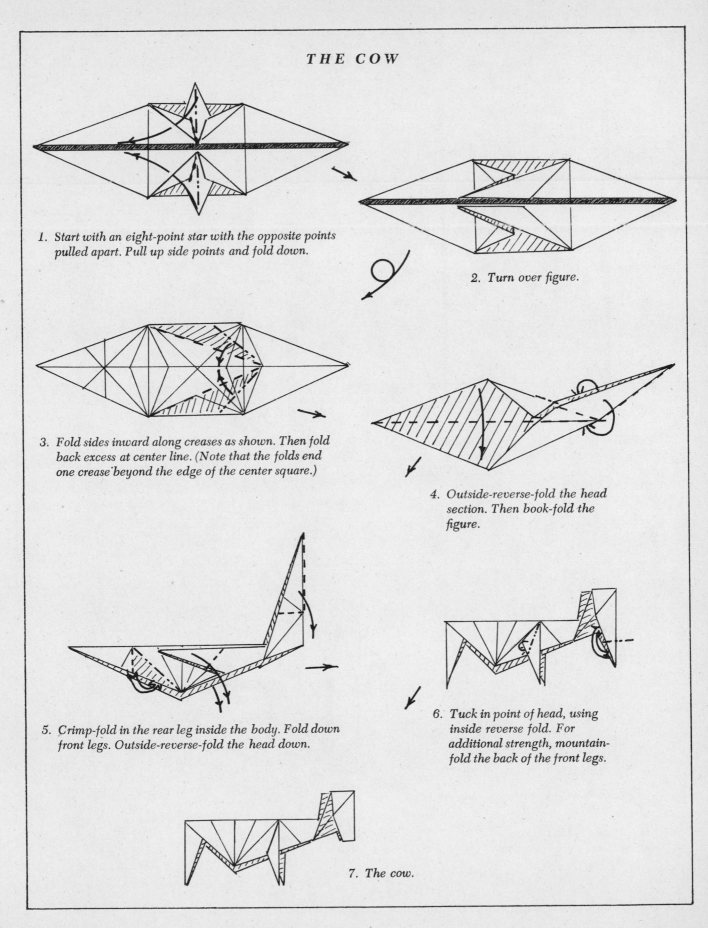

1. Start with an eight-point star with the opposite points pulled apart. Pull up side points and fold down.

2. Turn over figure.

3. Fold sides inward along creases as shown. Then fold back excess at center line. (Note that the folds end one crease beyond the edge of the center square.)

4. Outside-reverse-fold the head section. Then book-fold the figure.

5. Crimp-fold in the rear leg inside the body. Fold down front legs. Outside-reverse-fold the head down.

6. Tuck in point of head, using inside reverse fold. For additional strength, mountain-fold the back of the front legs.

7. The cow.

# THE NUN

The beginning steps are those for the cow, except for the position of the side points. Fold the cow before trying the nun.

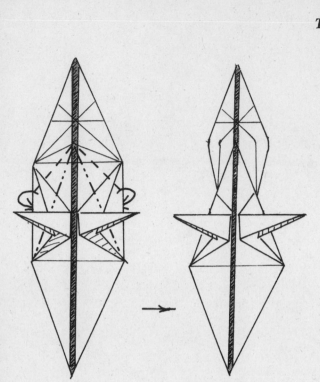

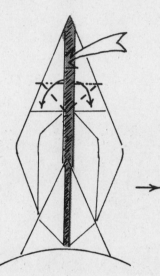

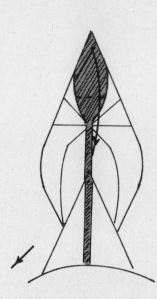

1. *Pull apart opposite flaps of an eight-point star. Then rearrange the short side points as shown here. Mountain-fold the sides and fold back excess at center line.*

2. *Open out head section. Fold down raw edges along creases.*

3. *Compound-fold: Continue folding down raw edges and fold down tip of head section and squash down.*

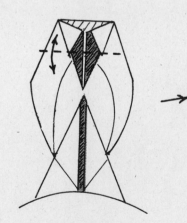

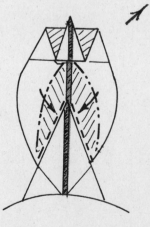

4. *Fold in sides to form face, with uncolored sides showing.*

5. *Make a crease by folding down head on top of face, using horizontal crease.*

6. *Loosen up head section and flip over from the back to the front of the body, using outside reverse fold. Fold head down against sides of hood.*

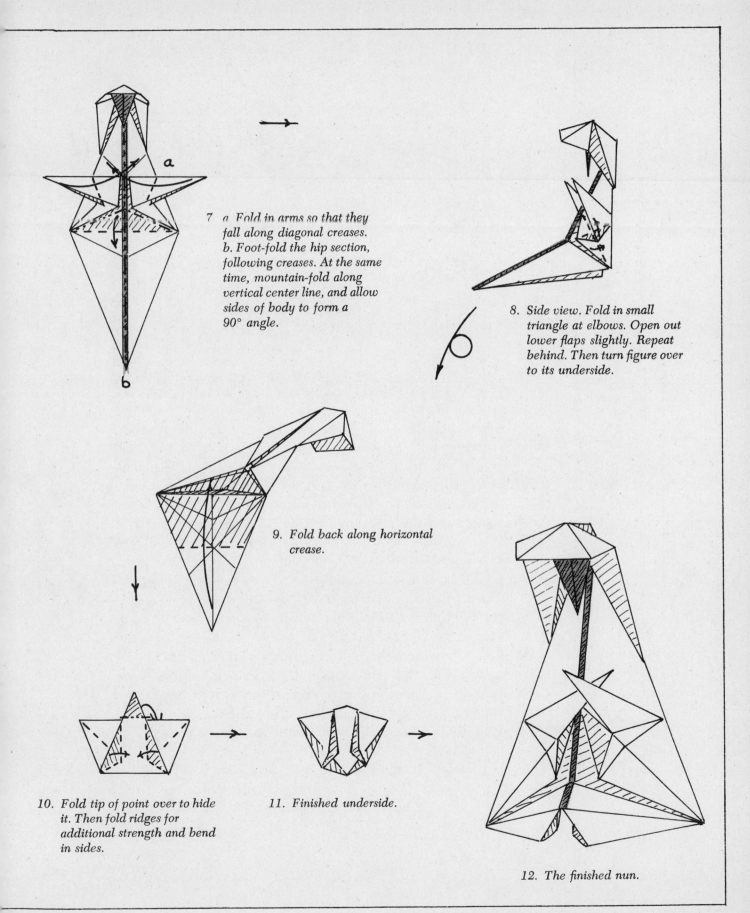

7  *a  Fold in arms so that they
fall along diagonal creases.
b. Foot-fold the hip section,
following creases. At the same
time, mountain-fold along
vertical center line, and allow
sides of body to form a
90° angle.*

8.  *Side view. Fold in small
triangle at elbows. Open out
lower flaps slightly. Repeat
behind. Then turn figure over
to its underside.*

9.  *Fold back along horizontal
crease.*

10.  *Fold tip of point over to hide
it. Then fold ridges for
additional strength and bend
in sides.*

11.  *Finished underside.*

12.  *The finished nun.*

# CHAPTER VI

# The T-Fold

The T-fold is made by pulling an eight-point star apart and making one of the long flaps perpendicular to the other. In this process the sides of the center square are kept folded in. From this are made two three-legged animals, the giraffe and the donkey, and the peacock. The giraffe, with its emphasis on long straight lines and stylized form, was my first artistic model. The donkey has an elaborate accordion fold to form the ears. It is sad in appearance; it is more attractive when viewed from the front rather than the side. However, it does not equal the elephant (not included in this volume) in attractiveness. The elegance of the peacock rests as much on the shape of the head as it does on the spreading tail feathers. Use of foil paper is necessary for the head. Both the donkey and the peacock use rabbit-ear folds to narrow down the legs.

The fox utilizes a T-form, but it starts, not with an eight-point star, but with an X-form base. This is achieved by folding the sides of the center square outward rather than inward and also more deeply than one would for the eight-point star. The result is that the center square takes on an hourglass figure, and the modified T-form falls at a downward angle rather than perpendicular to the main vertical flap. Narrowing of the body gives the fox its elegant appearance. It also features the characteristic animal snout, using a rabbit-ear fold.

The camel starts with an eight-point star and employs a T-shape in which both flaps open in the reverse direction from the T-fold shown opposite. This permits the formation of the camel's hump and the odd-shaped neck.

# THE T-FOLD

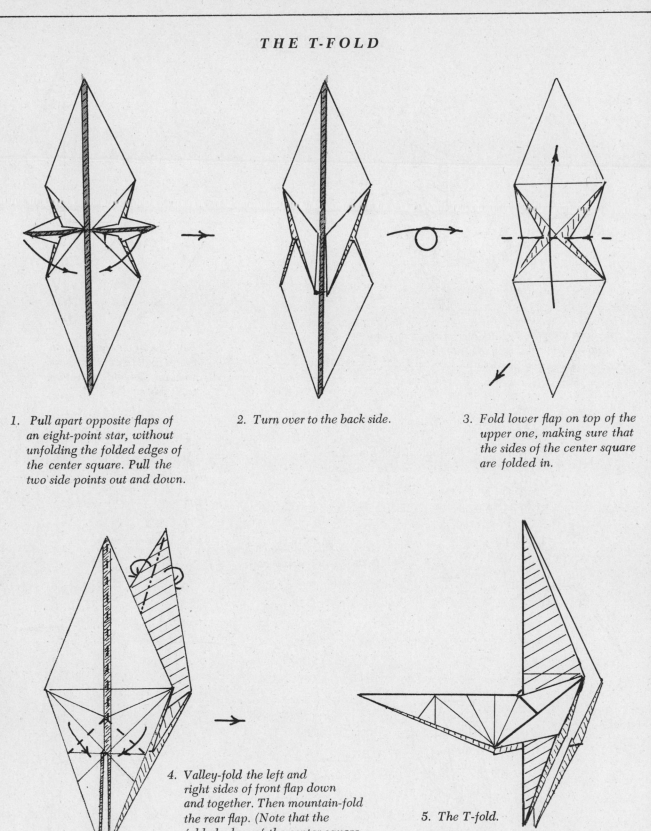

1. Pull apart opposite flaps of an eight-point star, without unfolding the folded edges of the center square. Pull the two side points out and down.

2. Turn over to the back side.

3. Fold lower flap on top of the upper one, making sure that the sides of the center square are folded in.

4. Valley-fold the left and right sides of front flap down and together. Then mountain-fold the rear flap. (Note that the folded edges of the center square go on the outside.)

5. The T-fold.

# THE GIRAFFE

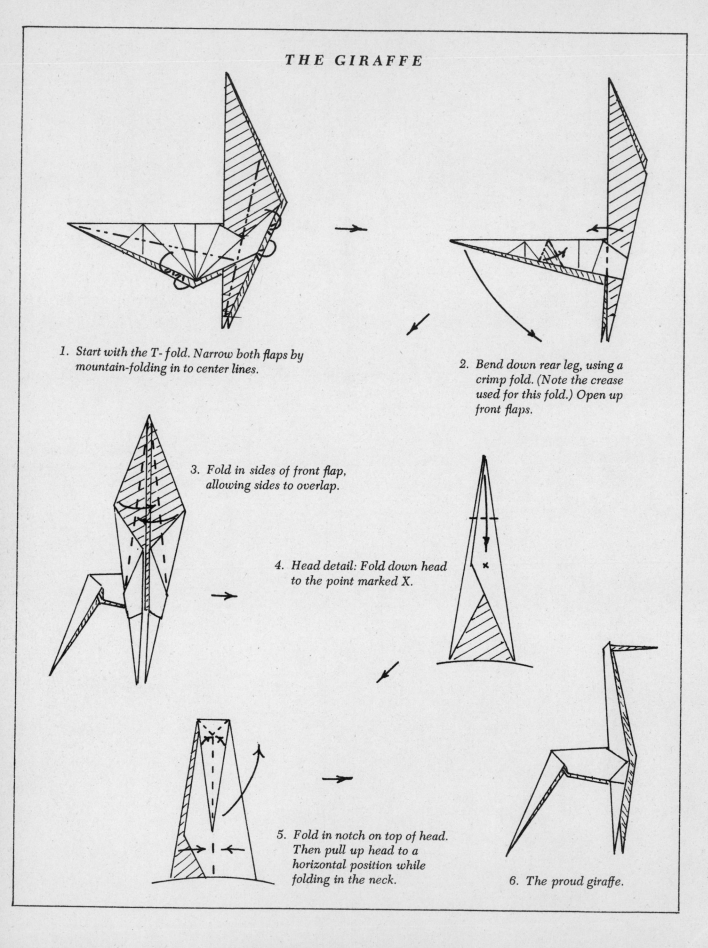

1. Start with the T-fold. Narrow both flaps by mountain-folding in to center lines.

2. Bend down rear leg, using a crimp fold. (Note the crease used for this fold.) Open up front flaps.

3. Fold in sides of front flap, allowing sides to overlap.

4. Head detail: Fold down head to the point marked X.

5. Fold in notch on top of head. Then pull up head to a horizontal position while folding in the neck.

6. The proud giraffe.

THE GIRAFFE        THE PEACOCK

THE FOX        THE DONKEY        THE CAMEL

# THE DONKEY

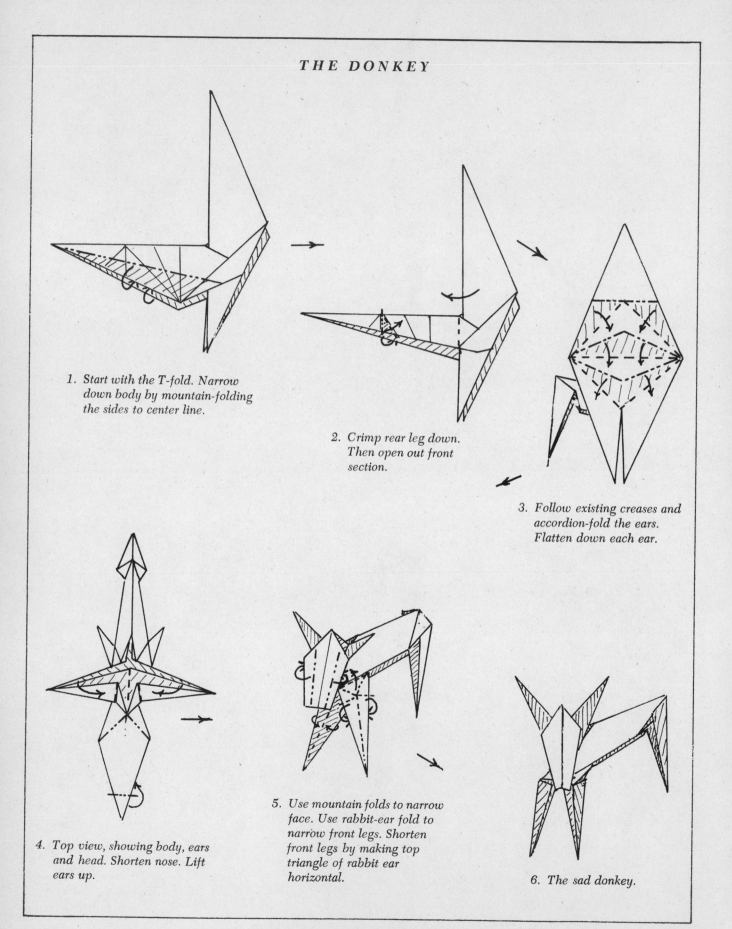

1. Start with the T-fold. Narrow down body by mountain-folding the sides to center line.

2. Crimp rear leg down. Then open out front section.

3. Follow existing creases and accordion-fold the ears. Flatten down each ear.

4. Top view, showing body, ears and head. Shorten nose. Lift ears up.

5. Use mountain folds to narrow face. Use rabbit-ear fold to narrow front legs. Shorten front legs by making top triangle of rabbit ear horizontal.

6. The sad donkey.

# THE PEACOCK

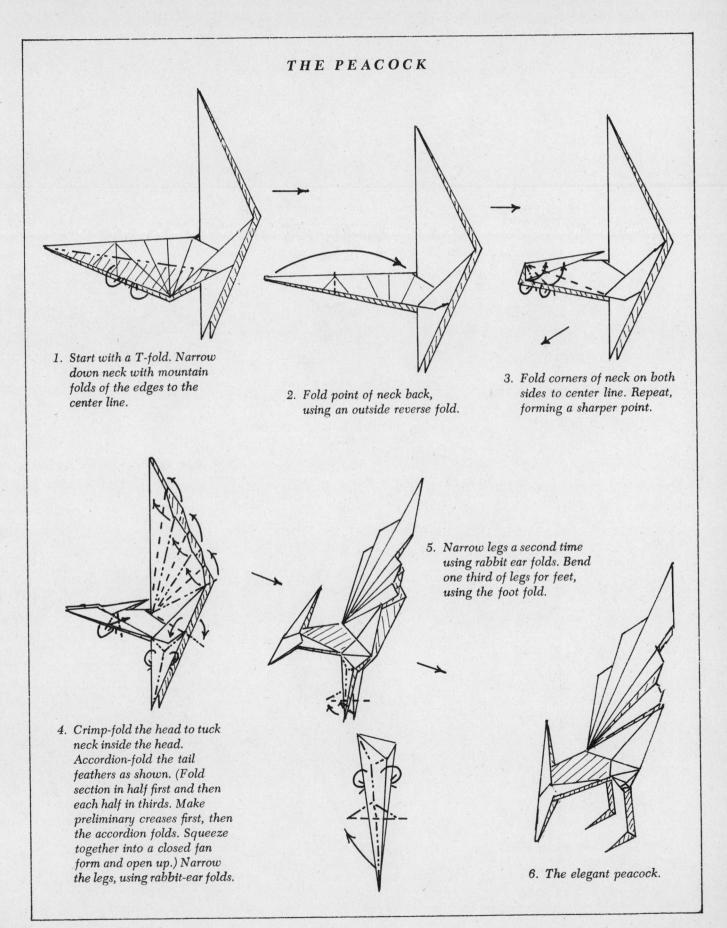

1. Start with a T-fold. Narrow down neck with mountain folds of the edges to the center line.

2. Fold point of neck back, using an outside reverse fold.

3. Fold corners of neck on both sides to center line. Repeat, forming a sharper point.

4. Crimp-fold the head to tuck neck inside the head. Accordion-fold the tail feathers as shown. (Fold section in half first and then each half in thirds. Make preliminary creases first, then the accordion folds. Squeeze together into a closed fan form and open up.) Narrow the legs, using rabbit-ear folds.

5. Narrow legs a second time using rabbit ear folds. Bend one third of legs for feet, using the foot fold.

6. The elegant peacock.

## THE FOX

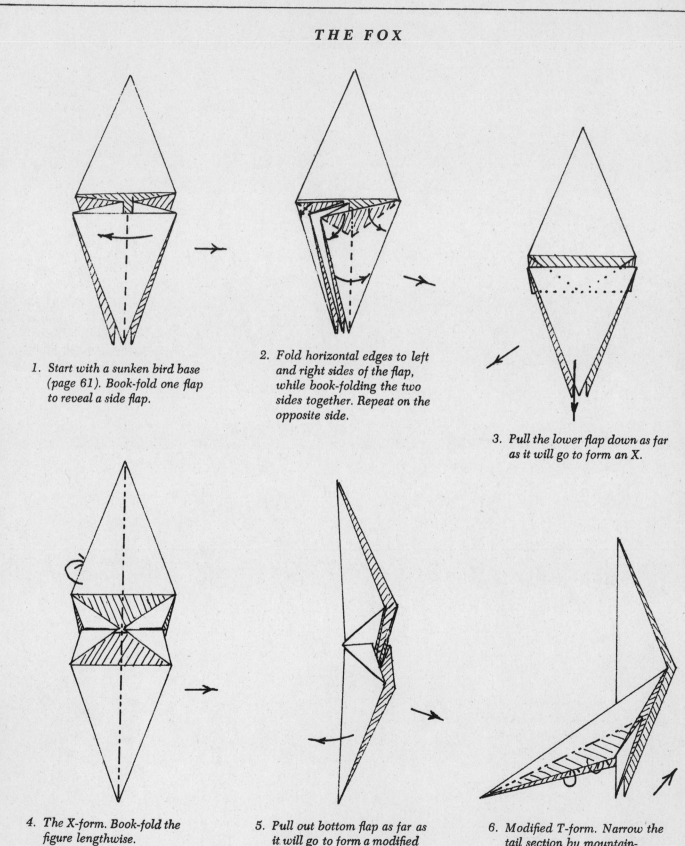

1.  Start with a sunken bird base (page 61). Book-fold one flap to reveal a side flap.

2.  Fold horizontal edges to left and right sides of the flap, while book-folding the two sides together. Repeat on the opposite side.

3.  Pull the lower flap down as far as it will go to form an X.

4.  The X-form. Book-fold the figure lengthwise.

5.  Pull out bottom flap as far as it will go to form a modified T-form.

6.  Modified T-form. Narrow the tail section by mountain-folding the sides to center line.

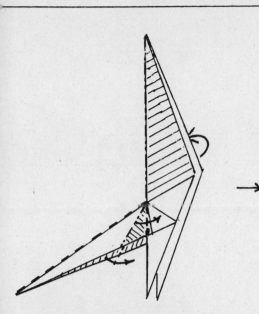

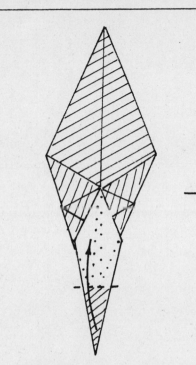

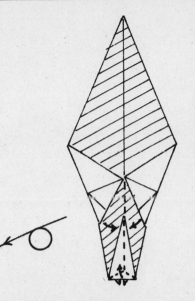

7. *Open out front section. Make a preliminary valley-fold crease on the base of the tail and squash down the tail flat.*

8. *Fold up tail even with bottom tips of front legs.*

9. *Fold in notch on bottom of tail. Squeeze tail section together and pull out tail at an angle.*

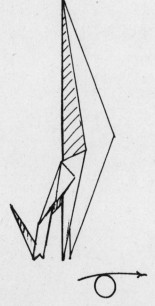

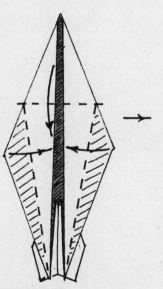

12. *Fold back notch to form ears. Then use rabbit-ear folds to form the nose.*

10. *Turn figure around to the front.*

11. *Valley-fold in the sides to center line. Then fold down head.*

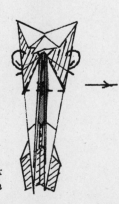

13. *Mountain-fold the neck back along triangle and fold down the triangle.*

14. *The fox.*

# THE CAMEL

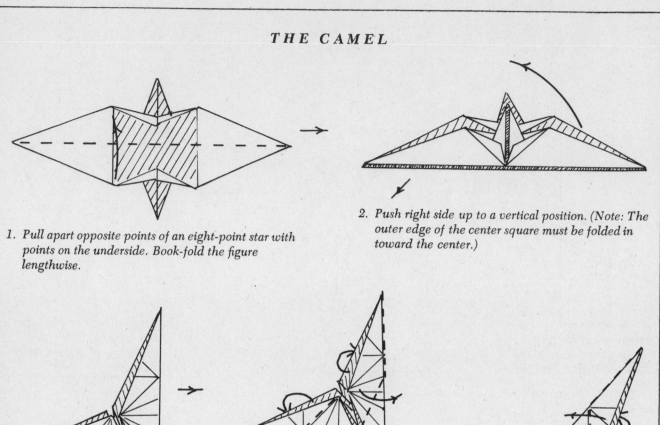

1. Pull apart opposite points of an eight-point star with points on the underside. Book-fold the figure lengthwise.

2. Push right side up to a vertical position. (Note: The outer edge of the center square must be folded in toward the center.)

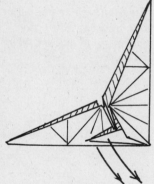

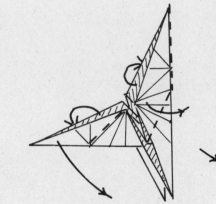

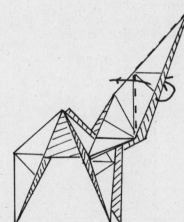

3. Pull out both side flaps.

4. Outside-reverse-fold the rear leg down. Outside-reverse-fold the neck forward.

5. Outside-reverse-fold the neck back again.

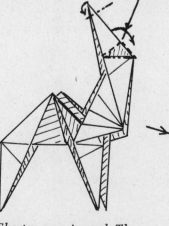

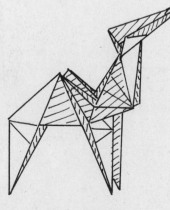

6. Shorten nose inward. Then fold head down, using a foot fold. (Sink triangular segment.)

7. The camel.

# CHAPTER VII

# Miscellaneous
# Eight-Point-Star Figures

Grouped in this chapter are a variety of figures based on the eight-point star which do not easily fit into other chapters. There are two human figures, King Tut and the bather, both of which employ the distinctive diamond-shape head. A lesson on the head is included in this chapter, since the head is used in many human figures. The trick lies not only in folding the diamond shape by means of accordion folds on both sides, but also in employing another accordion fold for the neck and shoulders. King Tut also employs the sitting position used by the nun. The bather represents my first timid attempt to fold a female figure.

The bat has been in the process of refinement over a period of years, and the final version is excellent. The head in particular required work to achieve its mouselike structure.

The swallow and the butterfly employ similar approaches. Both start with an eight-point star which is flattened out, and with the folding along existing crease lines begun. Both achieve a swallowtail effect and have a three-dimensional quality. The butterfly's body is given an accordion-fold treatment to achieve this three-dimensional effect.

In the mouse, and in the dachshund in the offset-center section (Chapter XI), the two short flaps are hidden and the four corners of the center square used as legs. Hiding a point is not the best practice, since it runs counter to the beauty of utilizing all of the points effectively. However, I consider it preferable to introducing cuts or even starting from a form other than a square. The mouse was developed in 1965, in contrast to most of the models in this book, which were created prior to 1962, and it shows the use of new moves, particularly in folding the head section. It has an attractive stylized form. Fred

Rohm, when shown the mouse, quickly adapted it so that it could be folded from a dollar bill.

To fold the penguin it is not necessary to fold the complete eight-point star. Its basic point of departure is turning two of the sides inside out to reveal the white underside in one of the flaps. While it was developed early, it underwent considerable experimentation to form the head. It is, of course, most attractive when made from dark paper with white on the underside.

*THE BATHER*          *KING TUT*

*THE BAT*

*THE SWALLOW*

# THE HUMAN HEAD

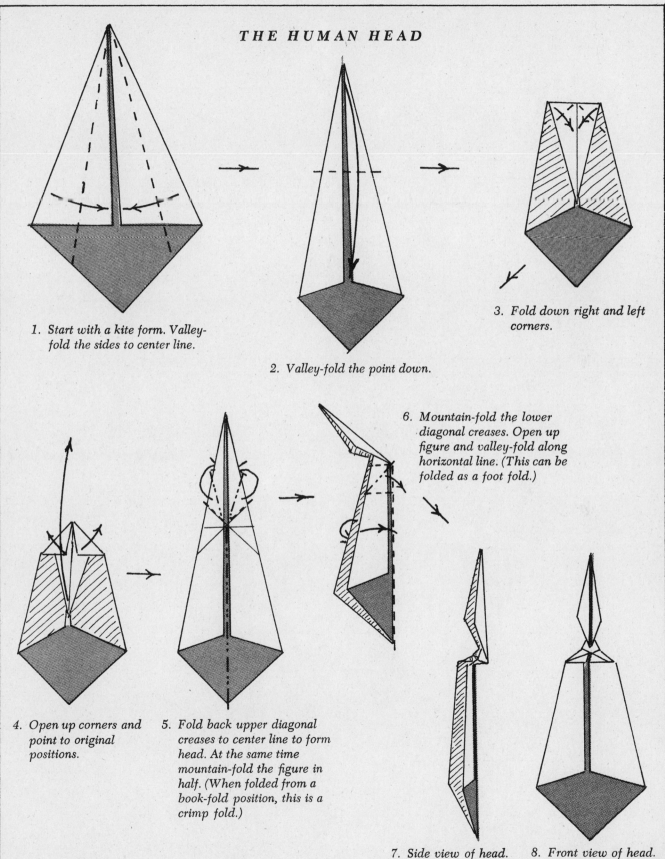

1. Start with a kite form. Valley-fold the sides to center line.

2. Valley-fold the point down.

3. Fold down right and left corners.

4. Open up corners and point to original positions.

5. Fold back upper diagonal creases to center line to form head. At the same time mountain-fold the figure in half. (When folded from a book-fold position, this is a crimp fold.)

6. Mountain-fold the lower diagonal creases. Open up figure and valley-fold along horizontal line. (This can be folded as a foot fold.)

7. Side view of head.   8. Front view of head.

## KING TUT

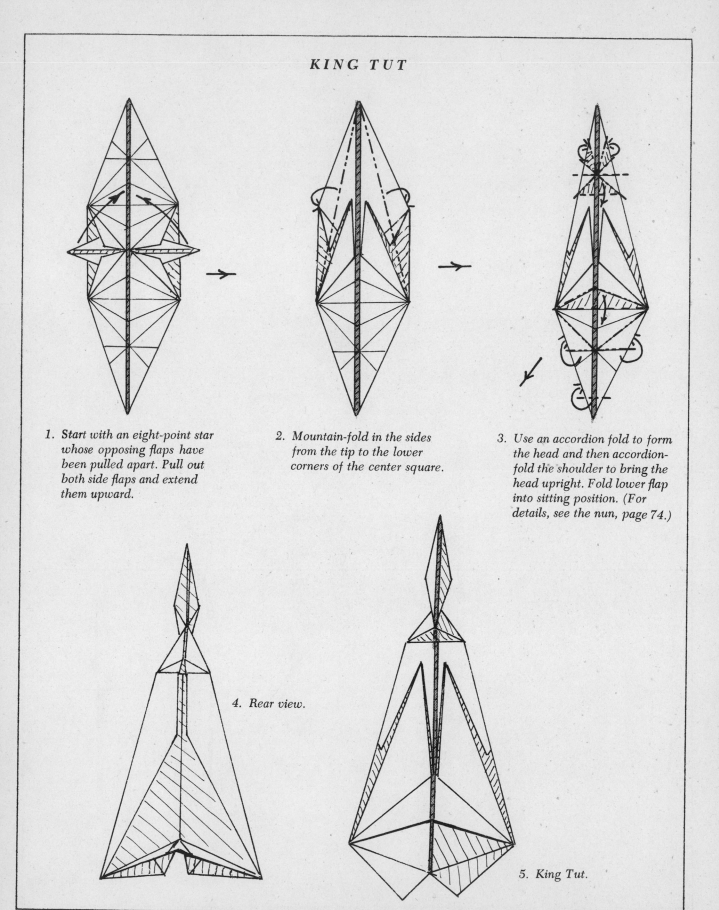

1. Start with an eight-point star whose opposing flaps have been pulled apart. Pull out both side flaps and extend them upward.

2. Mountain-fold in the sides from the tip to the lower corners of the center square.

3. Use an accordion fold to form the head and then accordion-fold the shoulder to bring the head upright. Fold lower flap into sitting position. (For details, see the nun, page 74.)

4. Rear view.

5. King Tut.

# THE BATHER

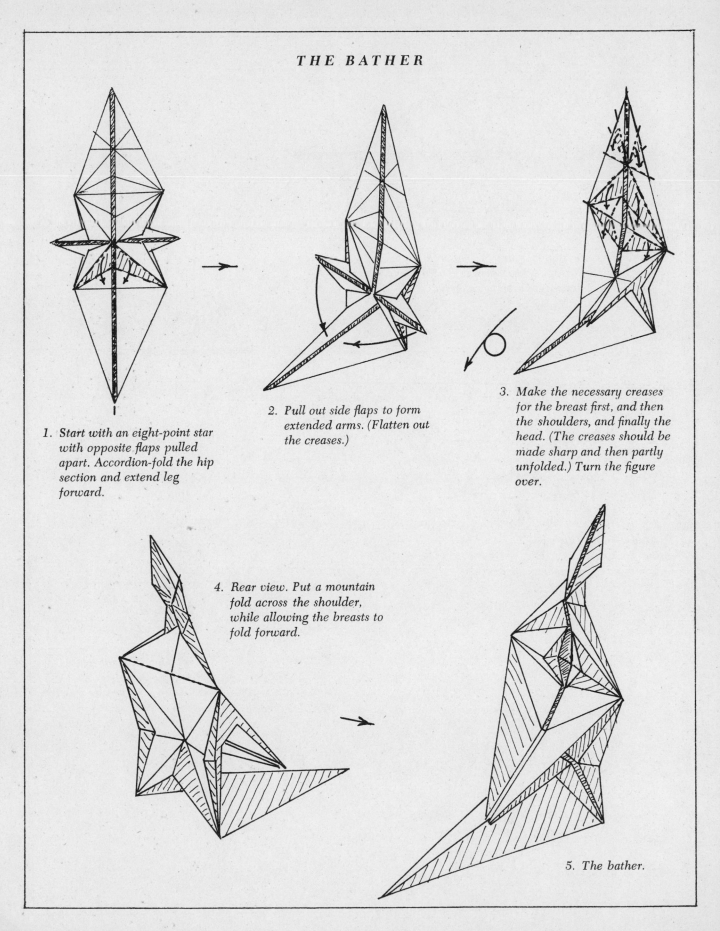

1. Start with an eight-point star with opposite flaps pulled apart. Accordion-fold the hip section and extend leg forward.

2. Pull out side flaps to form extended arms. (Flatten out the creases.)

3. Make the necessary creases for the breast first, and then the shoulders, and finally the head. (The creases should be made sharp and then partly unfolded.) Turn the figure over.

4. Rear view. Put a mountain fold across the shoulder, while allowing the breasts to fold forward.

5. The bather.

# THE BAT

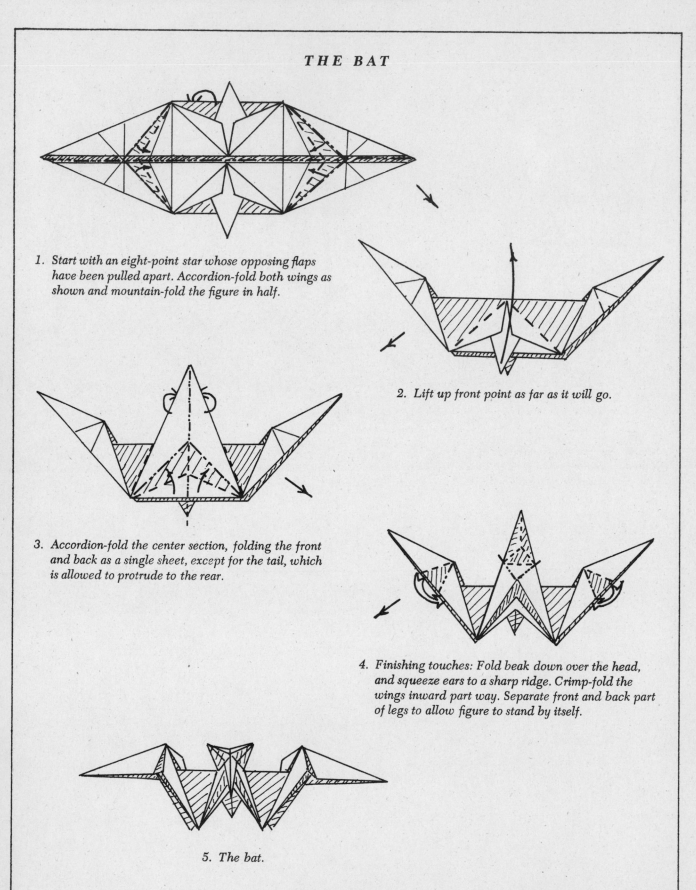

1. Start with an eight-point star whose opposing flaps have been pulled apart. Accordion-fold both wings as shown and mountain-fold the figure in half.

2. Lift up front point as far as it will go.

3. Accordion-fold the center section, folding the front and back as a single sheet, except for the tail, which is allowed to protrude to the rear.

4. Finishing touches: Fold beak down over the head, and squeeze ears to a sharp ridge. Crimp-fold the wings inward part way. Separate front and back part of legs to allow figure to stand by itself.

5. The bat.

# THE SWALLOW

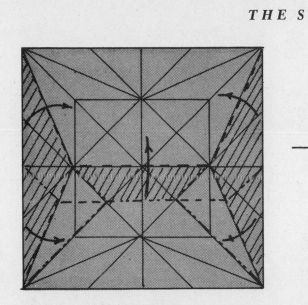

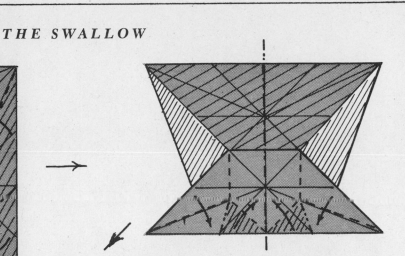

2. Valley-fold the raw bottom edge to the center line; then fold down sides. Mountain-fold the figure in half.

1. Start with the underside of an eight-point star which has been completely pulled apart. First make the mountain-fold creases. Then fold in the sides and squash down the center section.

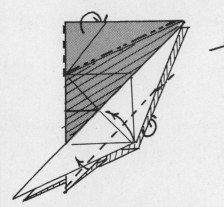

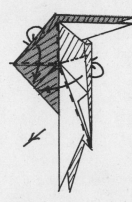

4. Rabbit-ear both points to form wings.

5. Valley-fold the side of the body and flatten down wing. Repeat behind.

3. Narrow down body section and tail together. Repeat behind. Inside-reverse-fold the upper edge.

6. Valley-fold the tails of the swallow. Accordion-fold the wings and spread out.

7. The swallow.

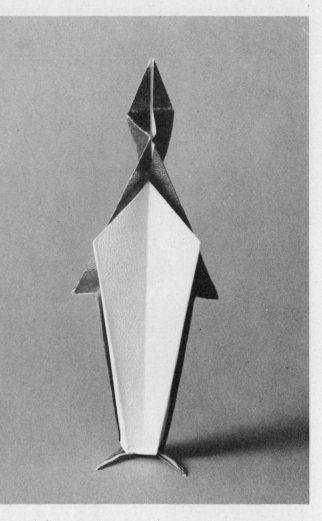

THE PENGUIN

THE SWALLOWTAIL BUTTERFLY

THE MOUSE

# THE SWALLOWTAIL BUTTERFLY

1. *Flatten out the center square of an eight-point star. Then pull out two corners with raw edges showing. Turn figure over.*

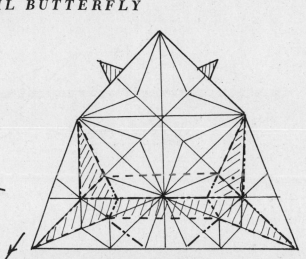

2. *First make the three horizontal creases, following a valley-mountain-valley order. Then accordion-fold the tails, following existing creases.*

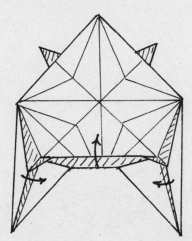

3. *Push down the raw edges of the center section and fold inward the outside edges of the tail.*

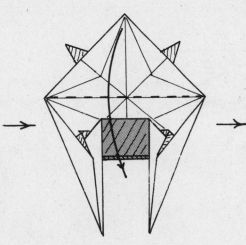

4. *Fold down front section.*

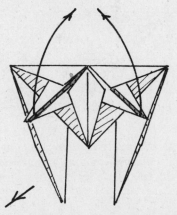

5. *Pull out antennas free of side flaps covering them.*

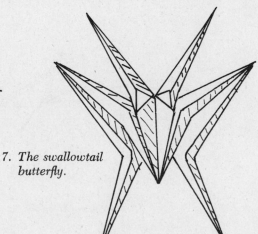

6. *Squeeze sides of antennas and swallowtails, using rabbit-ear folds. Then use an accordion fold to put valleys and ridges in the wings and the body.*

7. *The swallowtail butterfly.*

## THE MOUSE

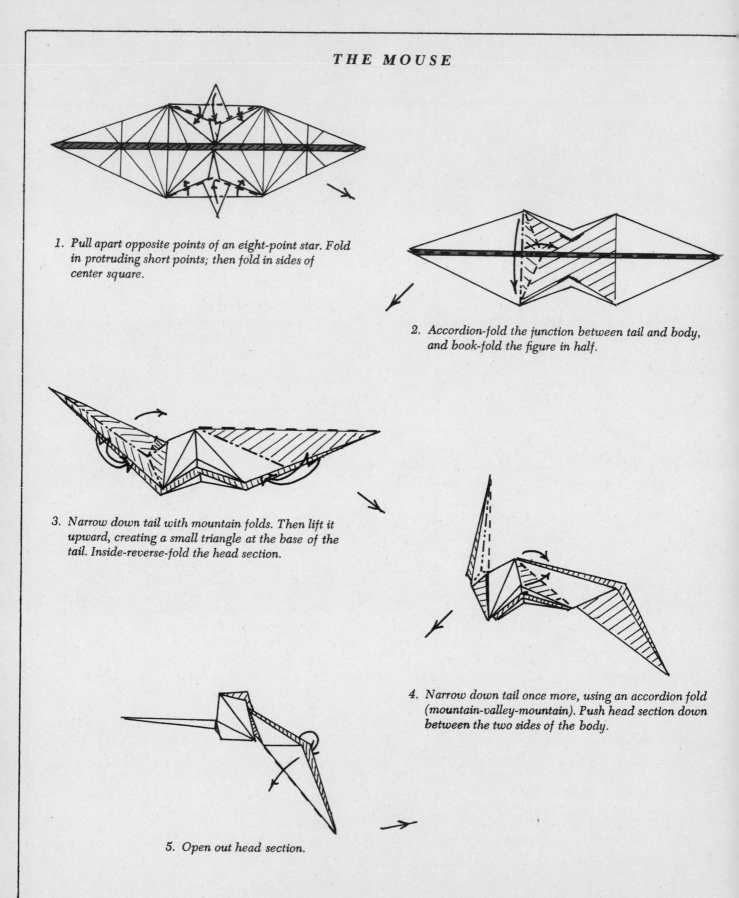

1. *Pull apart opposite points of an eight-point star. Fold in protruding short points; then fold in sides of center square.*

2. *Accordion-fold the junction between tail and body, and book-fold the figure in half.*

3. *Narrow down tail with mountain folds. Then lift it upward, creating a small triangle at the base of the tail. Inside-reverse-fold the head section.*

4. *Narrow down tail once more, using an accordion fold (mountain-valley-mountain). Push head section down between the two sides of the body.*

5. *Open out head section.*

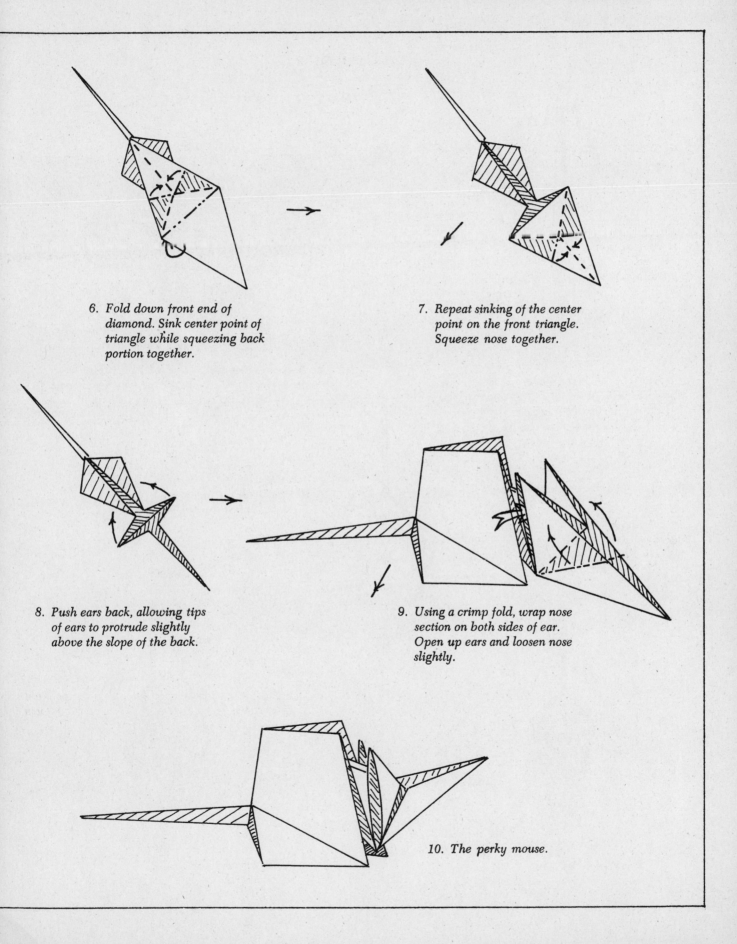

6. Fold down front end of diamond. Sink center point of triangle while squeezing back portion together.

7. Repeat sinking of the center point on the front triangle. Squeeze nose together.

8. Push ears back, allowing tips of ears to protrude slightly above the slope of the back.

9. Using a crimp fold, wrap nose section on both sides of ear. Open up ears and loosen nose slightly.

10. The perky mouse.

# THE PENGUIN

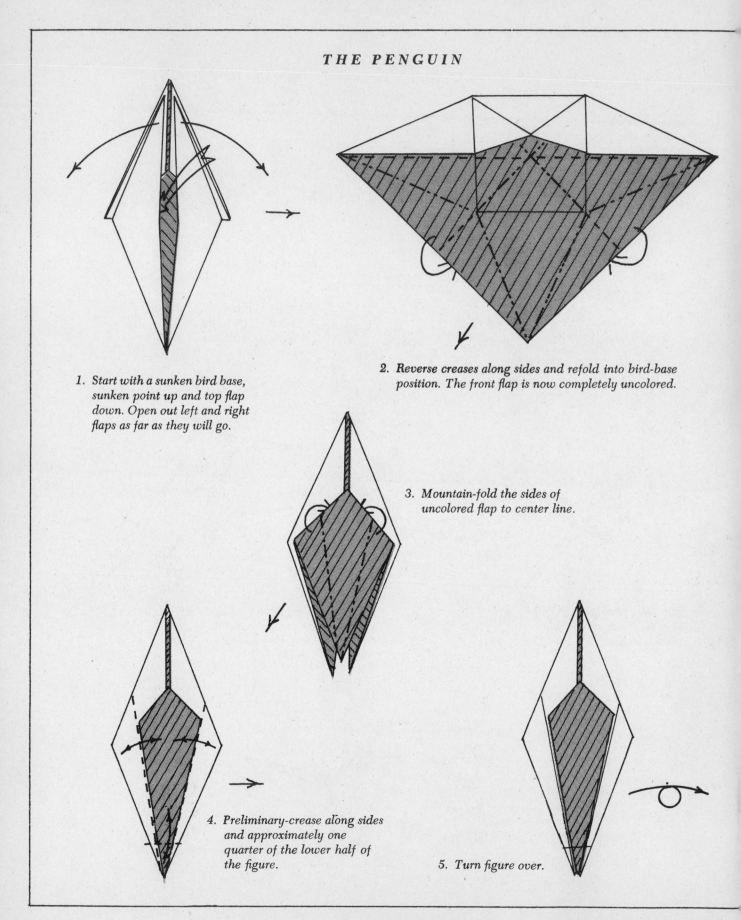

1. Start with a sunken bird base, sunken point up and top flap down. Open out left and right flaps as far as they will go.

2. Reverse creases along sides and refold into bird-base position. The front flap is now completely uncolored.

3. Mountain-fold the sides of uncolored flap to center line.

4. Preliminary-crease along sides and approximately one quarter of the lower half of the figure.

5. Turn figure over.

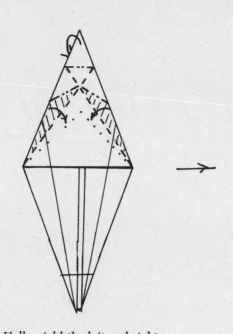

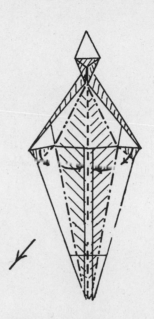

6. *Valley-fold the left and right edges to the upper edge of the hidden kite figure. Put in mountain-fold creases as shown. Shape diamond-shape head by folding together the ends of the pair of mountain folds and lifting the tip of the head upright.*

7. *Book-fold together the hidden white front. Then accordion-fold back as shown, and fold down flappers on each side. Turn sideways.*

8. *Tuck edges of white front into grooves made by the accordion fold.*

9. *Valley-fold both legs forward along preliminary crease line and fold back tail. (On the foot the colored portion is folded on top of the uncolored part.)*

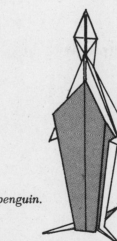

10. *The penguin.*

# CHAPTER VIII

# The Owl Base

The owl base starts with an eight-point star and ends up with two short side flaps, one short center flap and one long flap, and two corners of the center square. It thus provides six points in all. One of the less obvious steps in making the owl base is the locking in of the short center flaps. If the nose of the owl or the tail of the turtle is loose, the lock was not used properly.

The owl is undoubtedly the most universally admired of my foldings. It has a three-dimensional quality not equaled by any of the other figures. Considerable work went into development of the foot to enable the top-heavy figure to stand. When very large models are made it can be pasted against a board.

The lion, which was first created by my son, Bill, has been recognized as a dog as often as it has as a lion. Our most recent attempt to make it lionlike was to lift up its head.

The rabbit, with its beady eyes and its waistcoat, must certainly be considered to be the White Rabbit from *Alice in Wonderland*. In the monk, good use is made of the corners of the center square to form the legs; the figure has depth. The turtle achieves the remarkable effect of showing legs, tails and neck protruding from between its shells. The neck is formed by means of an elaborate accordion fold and is indeed thrust in between the shells.

THE MONK

THE RABBIT

THE TURTLE

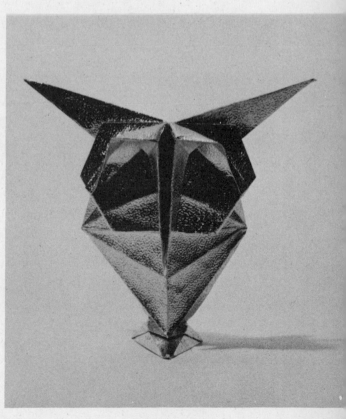

THE OWL

THE LION

# THE OWL BASE

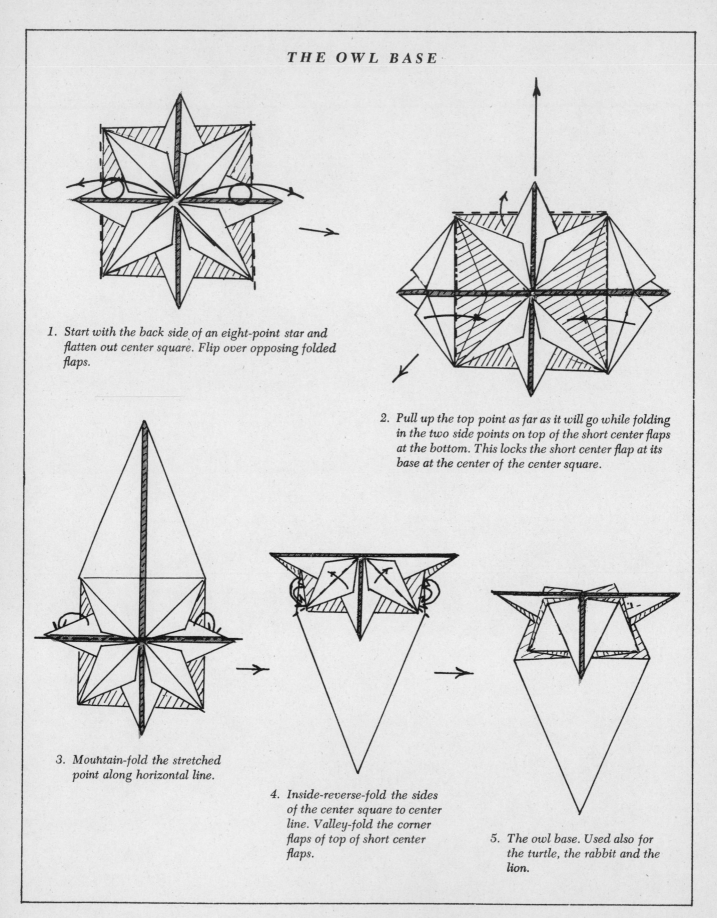

1. Start with the back side of an eight-point star and flatten out center square. Flip over opposing folded flaps.

2. Pull up the top point as far as it will go while folding in the two side points on top of the short center flaps at the bottom. This locks the short center flap at its base at the center of the center square.

3. Mountain-fold the stretched point along horizontal line.

4. Inside-reverse-fold the sides of the center square to center line. Valley-fold the corner flaps of top of short center flaps.

5. The owl base. Used also for the turtle, the rabbit and the lion.

# THE LION

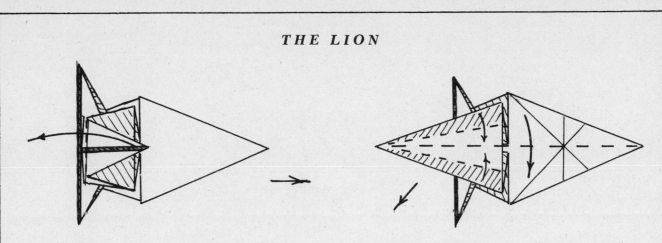

1. Start with the owl base. Lift up the center flap as far as it will go.

2. Narrow the tail section by valley-folding to center line. Then book-fold the figure.

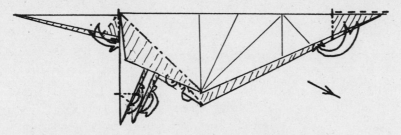

3. Crimp-fold the tail down, fitting the end of the tail inside the corner of the body. Similarly, crimp-fold the rear feet to the same length as the front one, then tuck in underside of body. Repeat behind. Blunt nose by inside reverse fold to vertical crease.

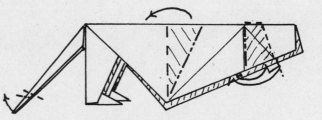

4. Open out front section. Crimp-fold the head outward toward back of body. Accordion-fold the face inward. Foot-fold end of tail.

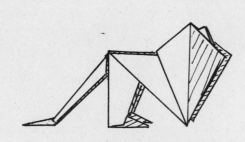

5. Lion by Bill Sakoda.

## THE OWL

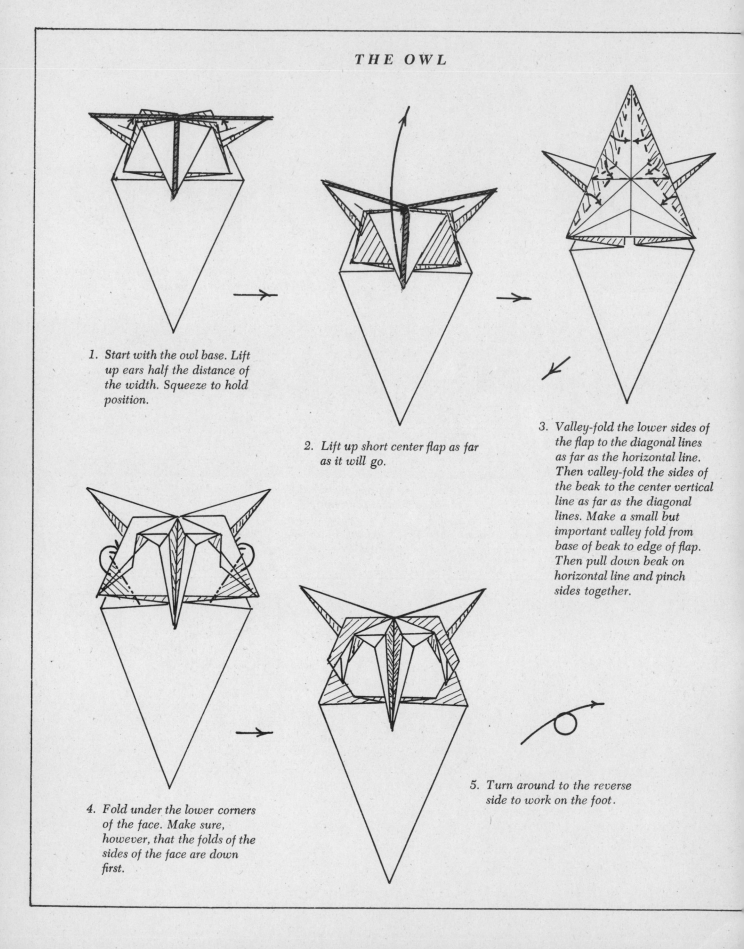

1. *Start with the owl base. Lift up ears half the distance of the width. Squeeze to hold position.*

2. *Lift up short center flap as far as it will go.*

3. *Valley-fold the lower sides of the flap to the diagonal lines as far as the horizontal line. Then valley-fold the sides of the beak to the center vertical line as far as the diagonal lines. Make a small but important valley fold from base of beak to edge of flap. Then pull down beak on horizontal line and pinch sides together.*

4. *Fold under the lower corners of the face. Make sure, however, that the folds of the sides of the face are down first.*

5. *Turn around to the reverse side to work on the foot.*

The owl's foot is also used in human figures.

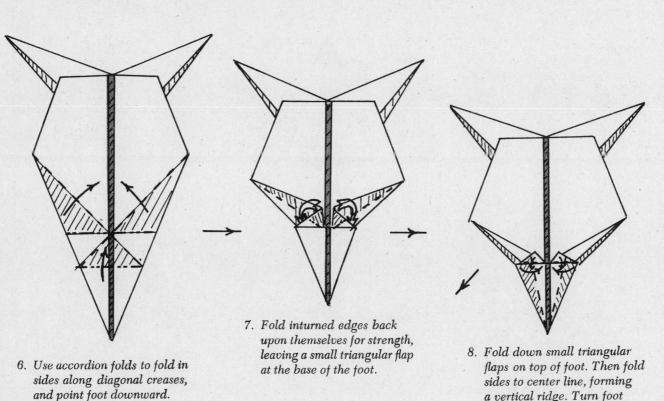

6. *Use accordion folds to fold in sides along diagonal creases, and point foot downward.*

7. *Fold inturned edges back upon themselves for strength, leaving a small triangular flap at the base of the foot.*

8. *Fold down small triangular flaps on top of foot. Then fold sides to center line, forming a vertical ridge. Turn foot forward and pull back sides of body to a 90° angle.*

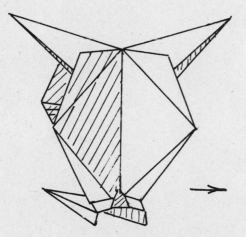

9. *Back of the owl. Note that the inturned edges are spread out. Mountain-fold the rear edge of the foot to add rigidity.*

10. *The owl.*

# THE RABBIT

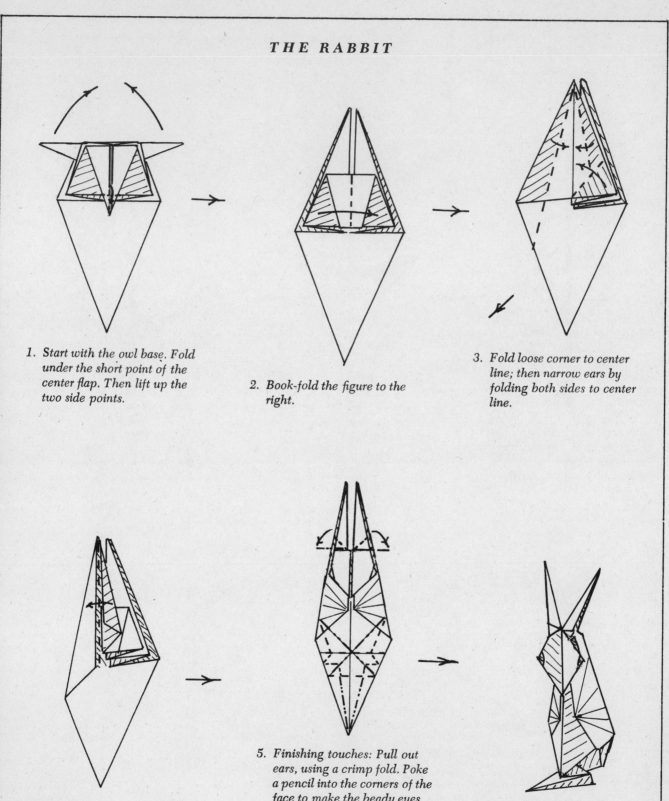

1. Start with the owl base. Fold under the short point of the center flap. Then lift up the two side points.

2. Book-fold the figure to the right.

3. Fold loose corner to center line; then narrow ears by folding both sides to center line.

4. Book-fold twice to the left and repeat Step 3 on the opposite side. Then return to center of figure.

5. Finishing touches: Pull out ears, using a crimp fold. Poke a pencil into the corners of the face to make the beady eyes more pronounced. Open out front of coat slightly. Form foot, following Steps 6–8 of the owl.

6. The White Rabbit.

# THE MONK

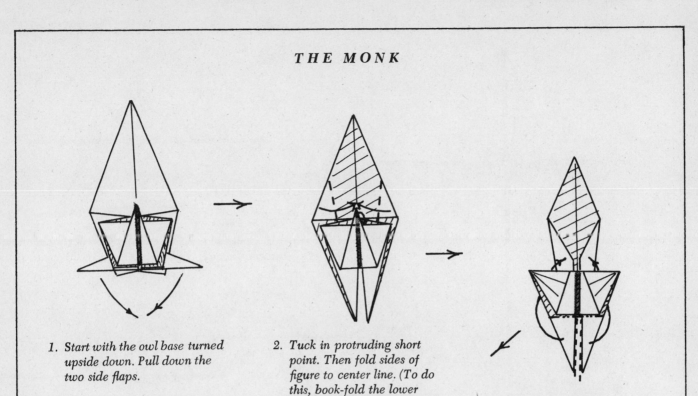

1. Start with the owl base turned upside down. Pull down the two side flaps.

2. Tuck in protruding short point. Then fold sides of figure to center line. (To do this, book-fold the lower halves of the figure on one side, then the other.)

3. Inside-reverse-fold the extended side flaps upward to form hands.

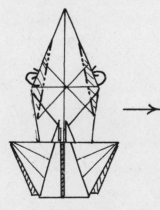

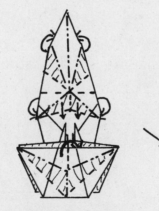

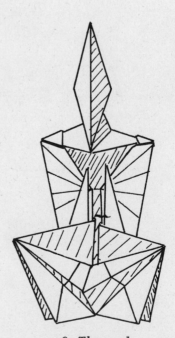

4. Fold under sides.

5. Use accordion fold to form head, and squeeze the head together. Then accordion-fold the shoulder downward, bringing the head upright. Finally, use accordion fold to form crossed legs. Loosen garment just behind uplifted hands to give the figure more depth.

6. The monk.

# THE TURTLE

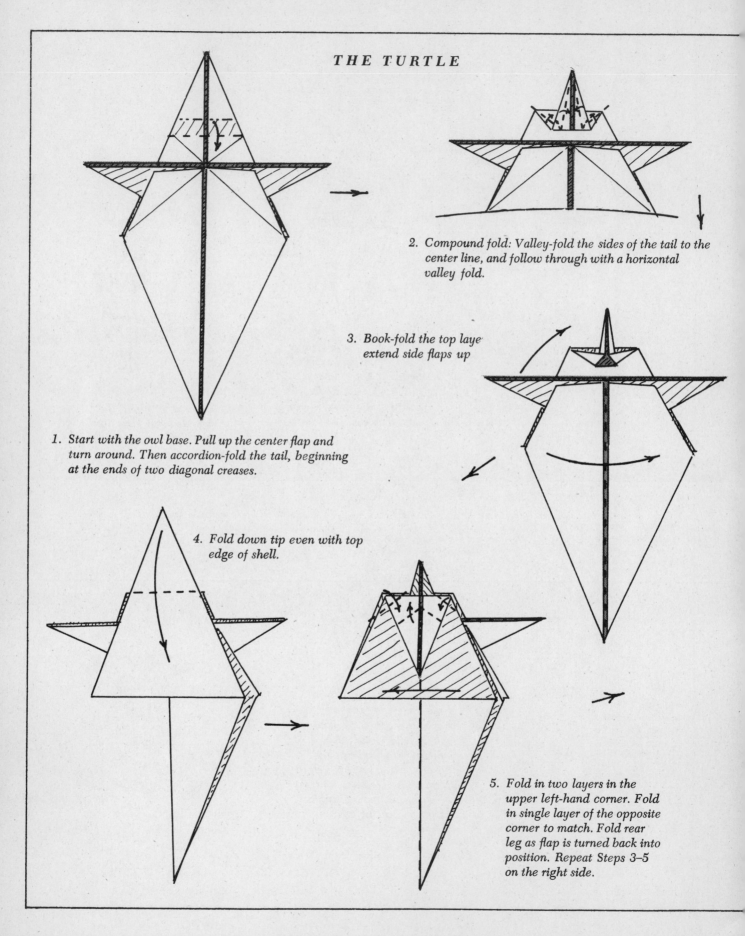

1. Start with the owl base. Pull up the center flap and turn around. Then accordion-fold the tail, beginning at the ends of two diagonal creases.

2. Compound fold: Valley-fold the sides of the tail to the center line, and follow through with a horizontal valley fold.

3. Book-fold the top layer; extend side flaps up

4. Fold down tip even with top edge of shell.

5. Fold in two layers in the upper left-hand corner. Fold in single layer of the opposite corner to match. Fold rear leg as flap is turned back into position. Repeat Steps 3–5 on the right side.

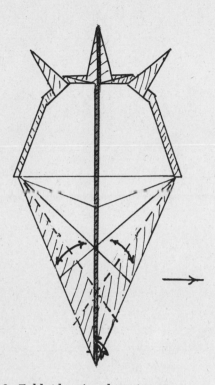

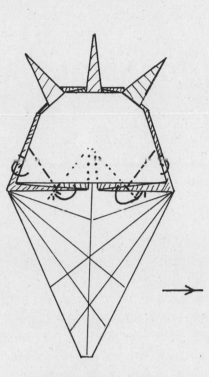

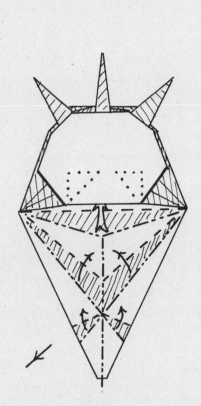

6. Fold sides of neck section to diagonal line; unfold. Tuck in short section at point of neck section. Then turn figure over.

7. Fold under the corners showing under the shell. Then fold under the corners of the shell.

8. Start at the tip and accordion-fold the head and the neck. Then tuck the base of the neck under the shell.

9. Finishing touches: Fold rear legs down. Fold front legs down, at the same time folding down sides of the body. Mountain-fold the tail and the shell.

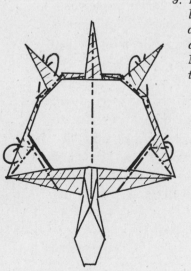

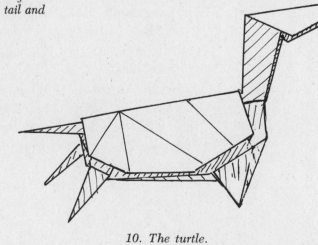

10. The turtle.

# CHAPTER IX

# The Stretched Bird Base

The stretched bird base has an effect similar to the bird base with a sunken point: the center point disappears. Instead of revealing the center square, however, the stretched bird base leaves two swinging flaps side by side. This makes possible the long legs of the standing crane. The legs and the neck of the crane are made to appear even longer by using foil paper and adding additional narrowing folds. More than any other figure, the standing crane reveals the beauty in long, straight and narrow limbs.

The beauty of the straight line is also evident in the praying mantis, but here it is the narrowing of the body which provides the straight lines bent at an attractive angle. The roadrunner is clearly a modification of the standing crane. The angle at which the legs are spread apart gives it a sense of motion and the comical appearance associated with the desert bird. The pelican is a modification of the praying mantis, with the exaggerated bill to help in its identification.

The two long flaps are folded outward to form the claws of the lobster. Similarly, in the crucifixion the two flaps are narrowed down to form outstretched arms; a bit of accordion-folding is necessary to form the narrow neck, to show the head hanging to one side. The Constant Tin Soldier, standing up straight on one leg, has the typical diamond-shaped head and the foot used in the owl. The two long flaps used to form the arms. Anyone interested in the source of the name should look up the story by Hans Christian Andersen. He would then look forward to the folding of the ballet dancer, which is shown later.

# THE STRETCHED BIRD BASE

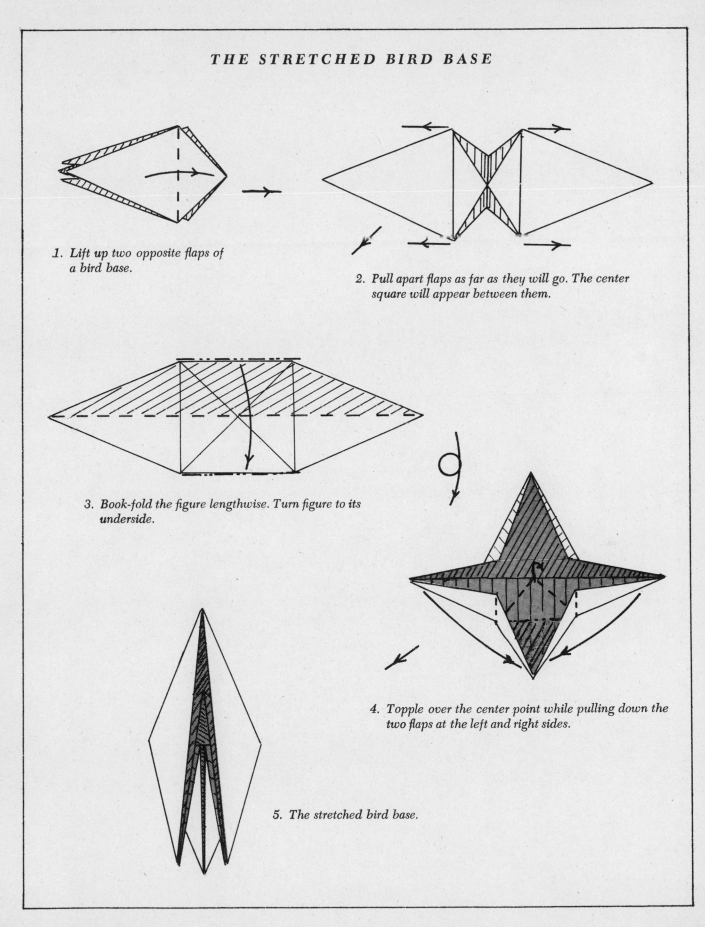

1. Lift up two opposite flaps of a bird base.

2. Pull apart flaps as far as they will go. The center square will appear between them.

3. Book-fold the figure lengthwise. Turn figure to its underside.

4. Topple over the center point while pulling down the two flaps at the left and right sides.

5. The stretched bird base.

THE PRAYING MANTIS

THE LOBSTER

THE STANDING CRANE

THE CONSTANT
TIN SOLDIER

# THE LOBSTER

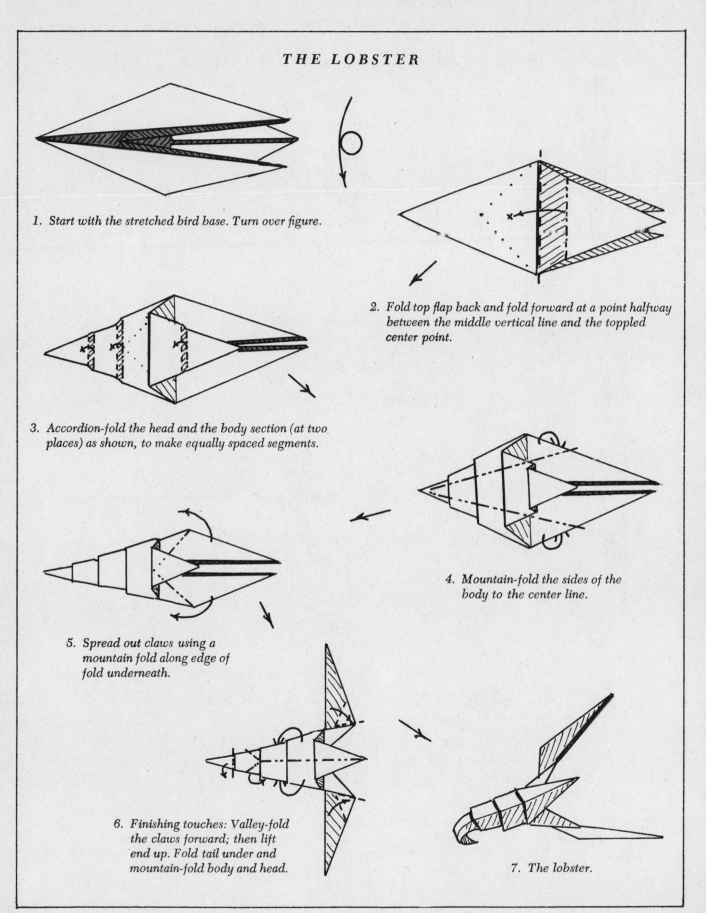

1. Start with the stretched bird base. Turn over figure.

2. Fold top flap back and fold forward at a point halfway between the middle vertical line and the toppled center point.

3. Accordion-fold the head and the body section (at two places) as shown, to make equally spaced segments.

4. Mountain-fold the sides of the body to the center line.

5. Spread out claws using a mountain fold along edge of fold underneath.

6. Finishing touches: Valley-fold the claws forward; then lift end up. Fold tail under and mountain-fold body and head.

7. The lobster.

## THE CONSTANT TIN SOLDIER

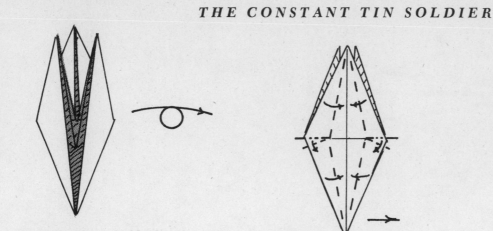

1. *Turn over a stretched bird base.*

2. *Valley-fold the lower edges to the center line. Then valley-fold the upper edges, including the loose flaps, to the center line. Accordion-fold the overlap to enable the figure to lie flat.*

3. *Take one arm and pull out so that one half of the length of the arm clears the body. Then valley-fold arm. Repeat on other arm.*

4. *Book-fold the figure outward and then turn over.*

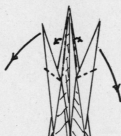

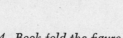

5. *Valley-fold soldier's right arm horizontally; left arm downward. Open out head section from the back. (Leave one layer on one side and two on the other.)*

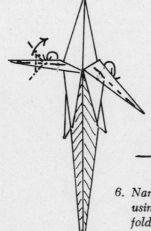

6. *Narrow down both arms, using mountain folds. Then fold soldier's right arm upward, using a foot fold.*

7. *Form head into sharp diamond shape using an accordion fold. Turn figure upside down and around to the back.*

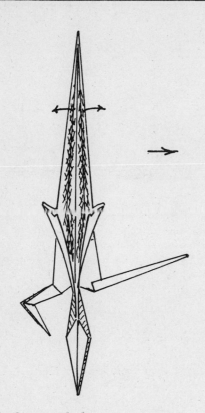

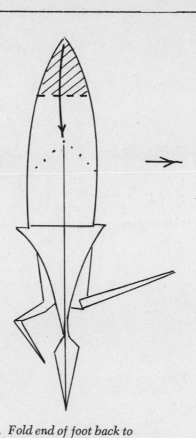

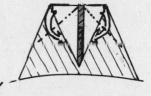

10. Fold corners to center line. Open up and slip under foot section.

8. Open up the bottom section of the figure from the back.

9. Fold end of foot back to toppled center of paper (invisible).

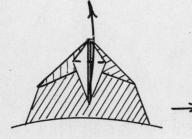

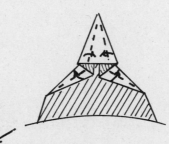

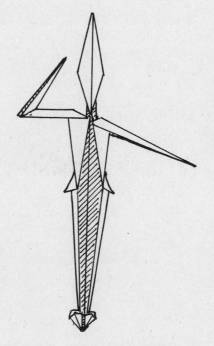

11. Fold over foot at its widest point.

12. Narrow down folded edge for additional strength. Fold sides of foot to center line; then open up to form a U.

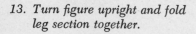

13. Turn figure upright and fold leg section together.

14. The Constant Tin Soldier.

## THE STANDING CRANE

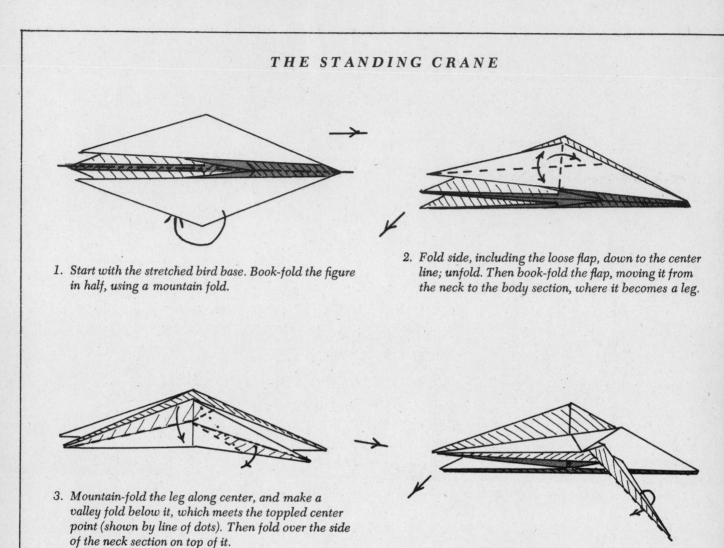

1. *Start with the stretched bird base. Book-fold the figure in half, using a mountain fold.*

2. *Fold side, including the loose flap, down to the center line; unfold. Then book-fold the flap, moving it from the neck to the body section, where it becomes a leg.*

3. *Mountain-fold the leg along center, and make a valley fold below it, which meets the toppled center point (shown by line of dots). Then fold over the side of the neck section on top of it.*

4. *Open underside of leg. The valley fold must extend down to the base of the leg.*

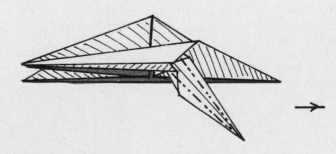

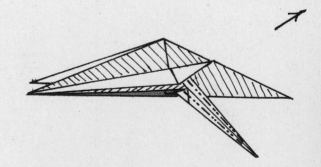

5. *Narrow down leg with mountain folds to the center line. (Preliminary creases with one's fingernail can be helpful.)*

6. *Narrow leg a second time. Then book-fold the sides of the leg together, with the folded edge facing the neck. Repeat Steps 2–6 on the reverse side to form the other leg.*

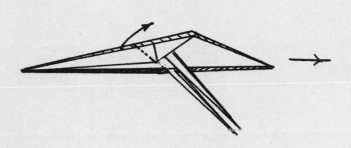

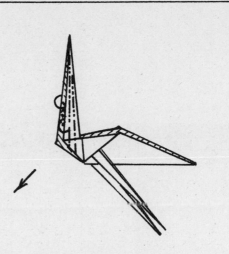

7. *Using the vertical crease on the base of the neck as a guideline, inside-reverse-fold the neck upward.*

8. *Narrow down neck by folding both sides into thirds, using mountain folds.*

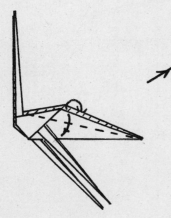

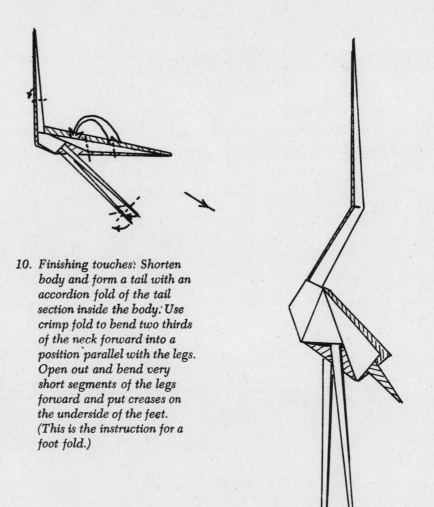

9. *Narrow down body by a valley fold of the top edge to the bottom.*

10. *Finishing touches: Shorten body and form a tail with an accordion fold of the tail section inside the body. Use crimp fold to bend two thirds of the neck forward into a position parallel with the legs. Open out and bend very short segments of the legs forward and put creases on the underside of the feet. (This is the instruction for a foot fold.)*

11. *The standing crane.*

## THE PRAYING MANTIS

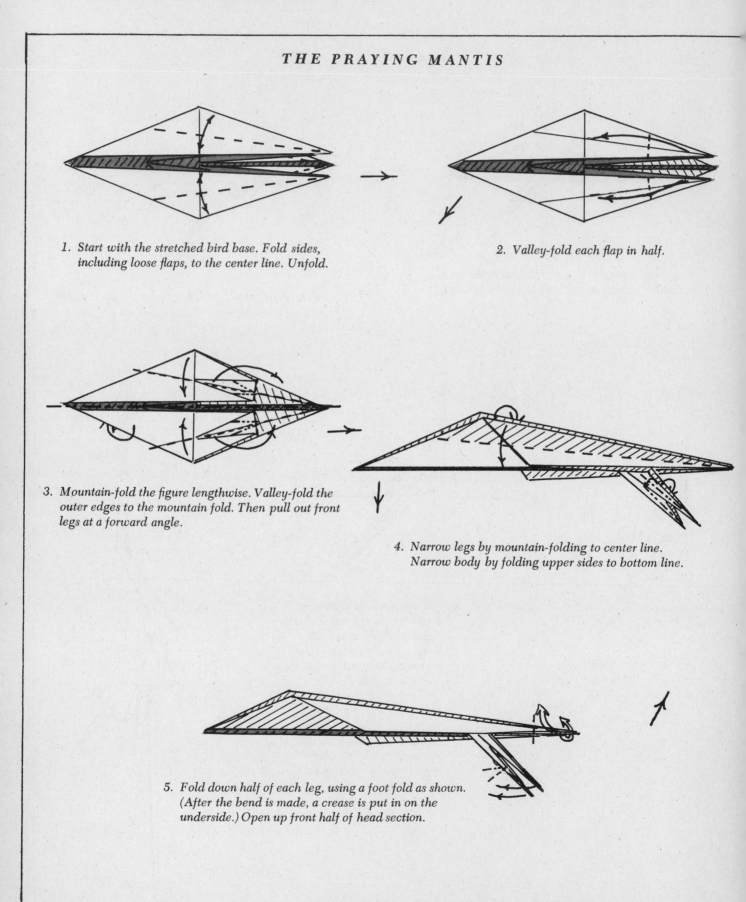

1. *Start with the stretched bird base. Fold sides,
   including loose flaps, to the center line. Unfold.*

2. *Valley-fold each flap in half.*

3. *Mountain-fold the figure lengthwise. Valley-fold the
   outer edges to the mountain fold. Then pull out front
   legs at a forward angle.*

4. *Narrow legs by mountain-folding to center line.
   Narrow body by folding upper sides to bottom line.*

5. *Fold down half of each leg, using a foot fold as shown.
   (After the bend is made, a crease is put in on the
   underside.) Open up front half of head section.*

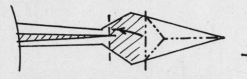

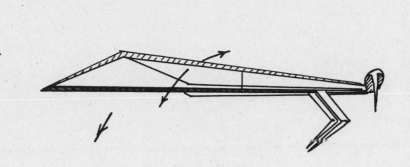

6. *Head detail: Lift up head section. Squeeze front end to form a point. Then bend it down, forming eyes at the same time. Bend head at a 45° angle toward the viewer.*

7. *Open out the back.*

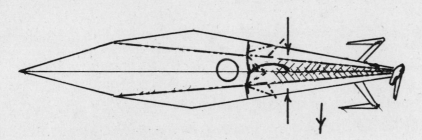

8. *Hold the body between fingers where the circle is placed. Then squeeze the front part of the body, at the same time pushing down at the point in front of the circle where the bend is made. (It is necessary to use some force to make this move, which gives the praying mantis its elegant appearance.)*

9. *The elegant praying mantis.*

# THE ROADRUNNER

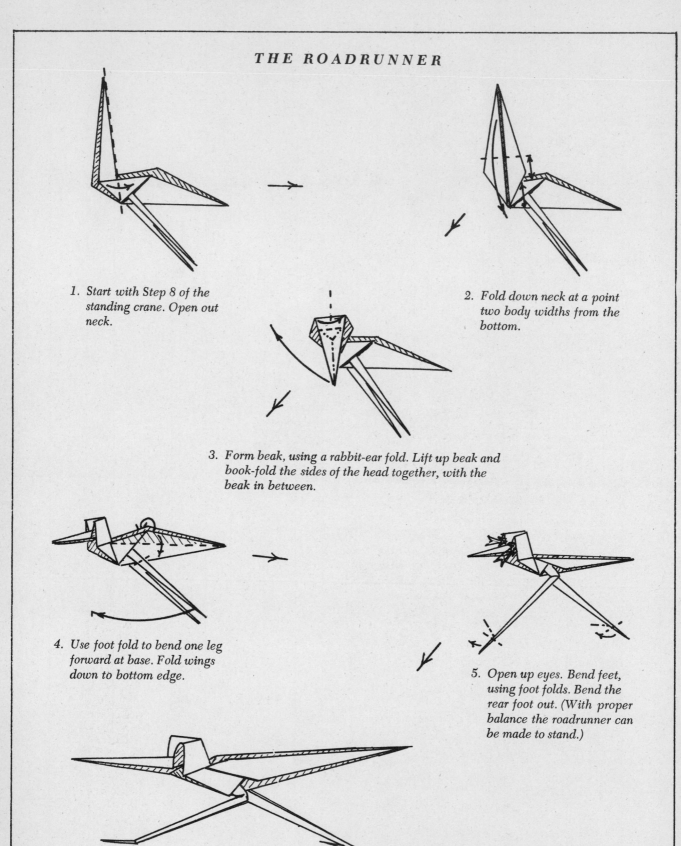

1. Start with Step 8 of the standing crane. Open out neck.

2. Fold down neck at a point two body widths from the bottom.

3. Form beak, using a rabbit-ear fold. Lift up beak and book-fold the sides of the head together, with the beak in between.

4. Use foot fold to bend one leg forward at base. Fold wings down to bottom edge.

5. Open up eyes. Bend feet, using foot folds. Bend the rear foot out. (With proper balance the roadrunner can be made to stand.)

6. The roadrunner.

THE ROADRUNNER

THE PELICAN

CRUCIFIXION

# THE PELICAN

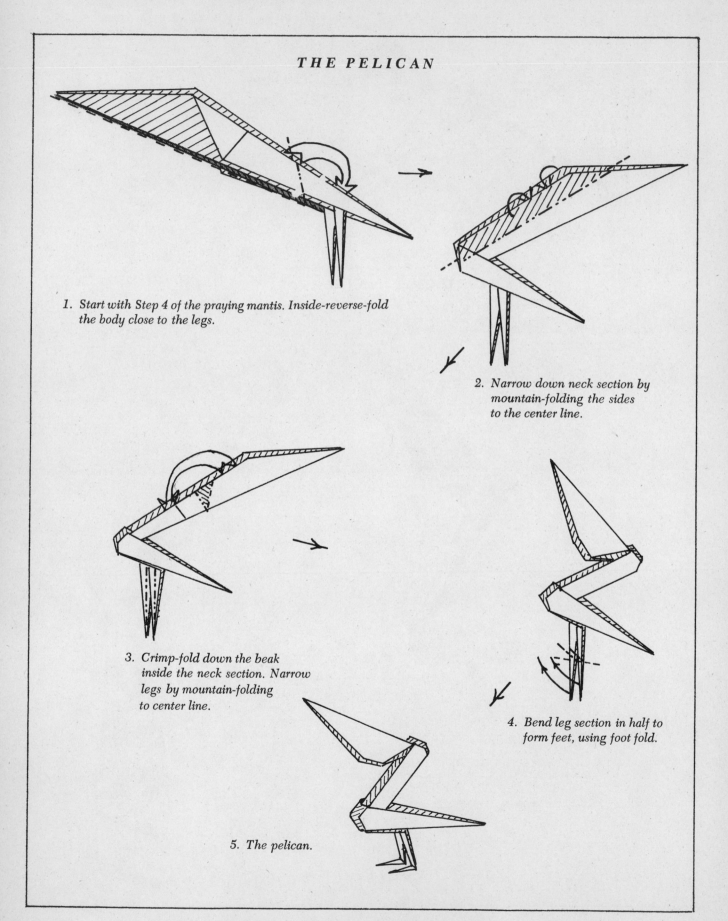

1. Start with Step 4 of the praying mantis. Inside-reverse-fold the body close to the legs.

2. Narrow down neck section by mountain-folding the sides to the center line.

3. Crimp-fold down the beak inside the neck section. Narrow legs by mountain-folding to center line.

4. Bend leg section in half to form feet, using foot fold.

5. The pelican.

# CRUCIFIXION

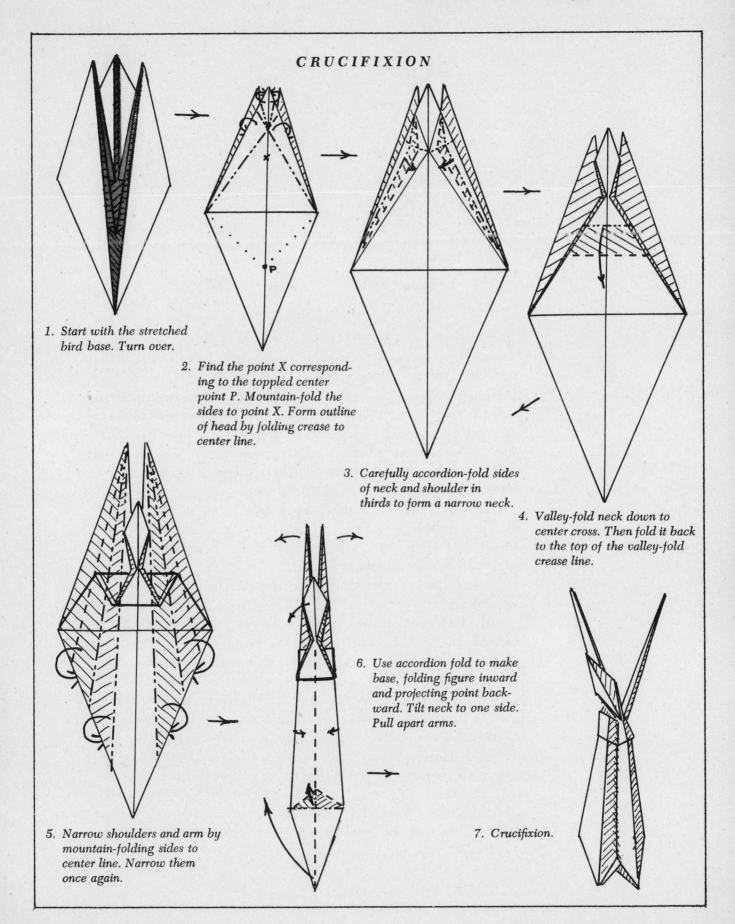

1. Start with the stretched bird base. Turn over.

2. Find the point X corresponding to the toppled center point P. Mountain-fold the sides to point X. Form outline of head by folding crease to center line.

3. Carefully accordion-fold sides of neck and shoulder in thirds to form a narrow neck.

4. Valley-fold neck down to center cross. Then fold it back to the top of the valley-fold crease line.

5. Narrow shoulders and arm by mountain-folding sides to center line. Narrow them once again.

6. Use accordion fold to make base, folding figure inward and projecting point backward. Tilt neck to one side. Pull apart arms.

7. Crucifixion.

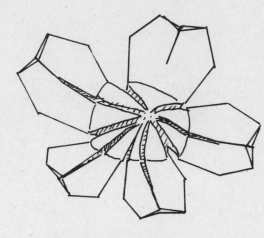

# CHAPTER X

# The Frog Base

The frog base is a neglected one; it is used to fold the traditional frog, but little else. Where the bird base has four points, the frog base has five, even though one of the points consists of many folds of paper. Only by using thin paper or foil paper is it possible to make adequate use of this fifth point. In the frog base the short triangular flaps can be left out or tucked under as needed. Tucking the short flaps under provides freer action for four of the flaps, an effect similar to that achieved for the stretched bird base.

The dragonfly was made after seeing the dragonfly in a reproduction from the *Kan no mado* which showed cuts to form the four wings. An analysis of the situation showed that five points could be easily provided by the frog base. The dragonfly features a compound fold which allows the narrowing of the wings and body simultaneously in one move.

The bulky stem is used as one of the petals to make the cherry blossom. The result is mystifying if one does not realize that this has been done. The five points make the frog base a natural one for human figures and the ape. The ape is folded in a squatting position, and the right arm is bent at the extreme so that it can be hung from a tree limb. As a matter of fact, it is possible to string several apes by hanging a second ape on the left arm of the ape above it. The skier and the ballet dancer are only two of the possible positions for human figures. Another possible position is that of a lumumba dancer. I once had a dancer standing on one leg, and the Constant Tin Soldier would have liked it. But it was a difficult position to maintain. As a matter of fact, to stand figures even on two legs requires some skill.

THE SKIER

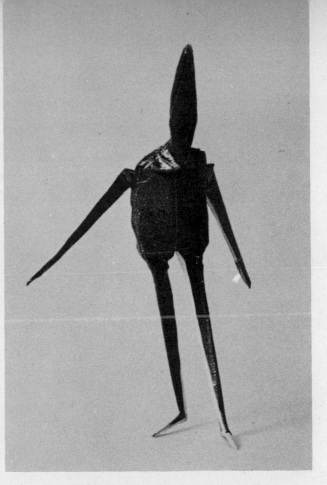

THE BALLET DANCER

THE CHERRY
BLOSSOM

THE DRAGONFLY

THE APE

# THE FROG BASE

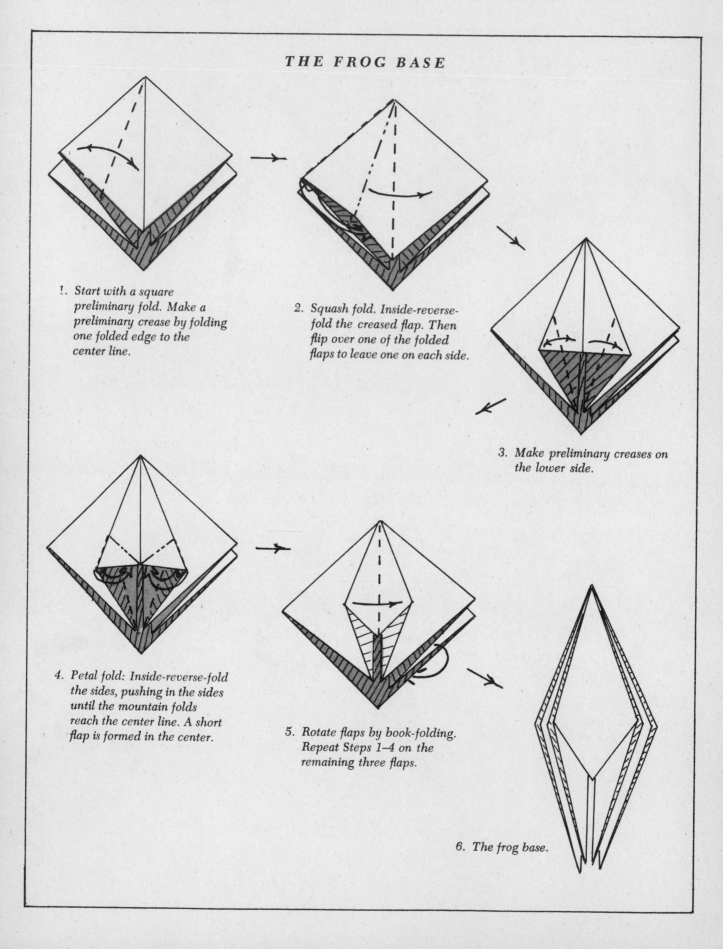

1. Start with a square preliminary fold. Make a preliminary crease by folding one folded edge to the center line.

2. Squash fold. Inside-reverse-fold the creased flap. Then flip over one of the folded flaps to leave one on each side.

3. Make preliminary creases on the lower side.

4. Petal fold: Inside-reverse-fold the sides, pushing in the sides until the mountain folds reach the center line. A short flap is formed in the center.

5. Rotate flaps by book-folding. Repeat Steps 1–4 on the remaining three flaps.

6. The frog base.

# THE DRAGONFLY

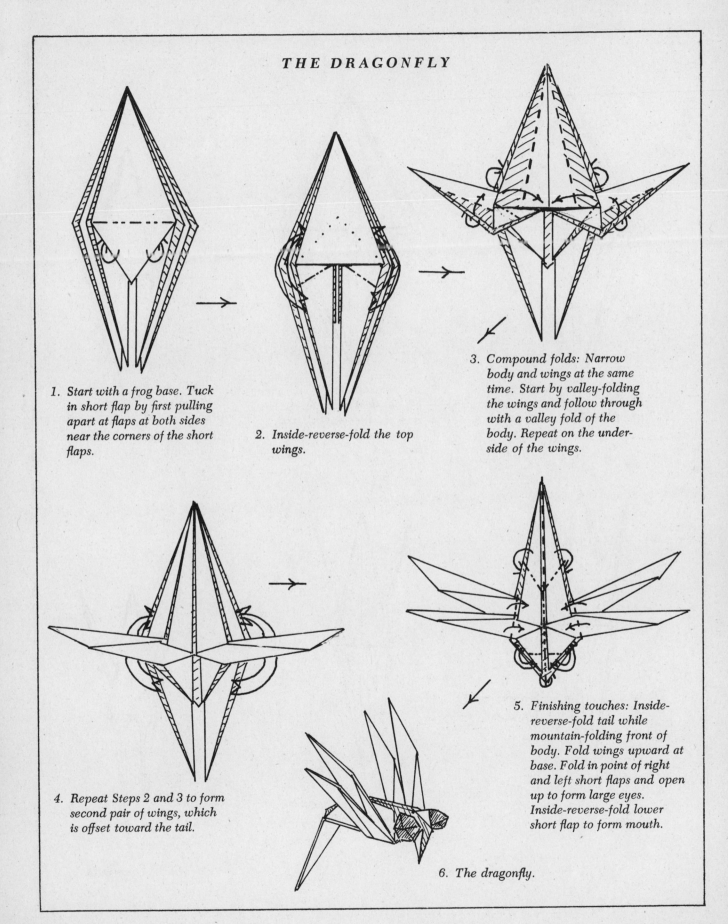

1. Start with a frog base. Tuck in short flap by first pulling apart at flaps at both sides near the corners of the short flaps.

2. Inside-reverse-fold the top wings.

3. Compound folds: Narrow body and wings at the same time. Start by valley-folding the wings and follow through with a valley fold of the body. Repeat on the underside of the wings.

4. Repeat Steps 2 and 3 to form second pair of wings, which is offset toward the tail.

5. Finishing touches: Inside-reverse-fold tail while mountain-folding front of body. Fold wings upward at base. Fold in point of right and left short flaps and open up to form large eyes. Inside-reverse-fold lower short flap to form mouth.

6. The dragonfly.

# HUMAN-FIGURE BASE

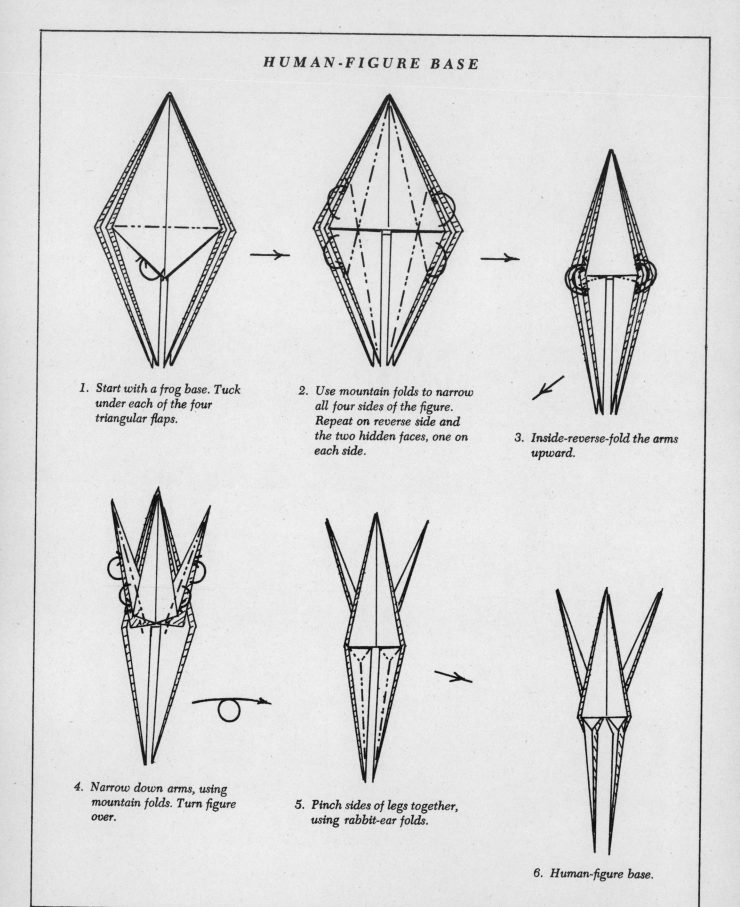

1. *Start with a frog base. Tuck under each of the four triangular flaps.*

2. *Use mountain folds to narrow all four sides of the figure. Repeat on reverse side and the two hidden faces, one on each side.*

3. *Inside-reverse-fold the arms upward.*

4. *Narrow down arms, using mountain folds. Turn figure over.*

5. *Pinch sides of legs together, using rabbit-ear folds.*

6. *Human-figure base.*

# HUMAN FIGURES

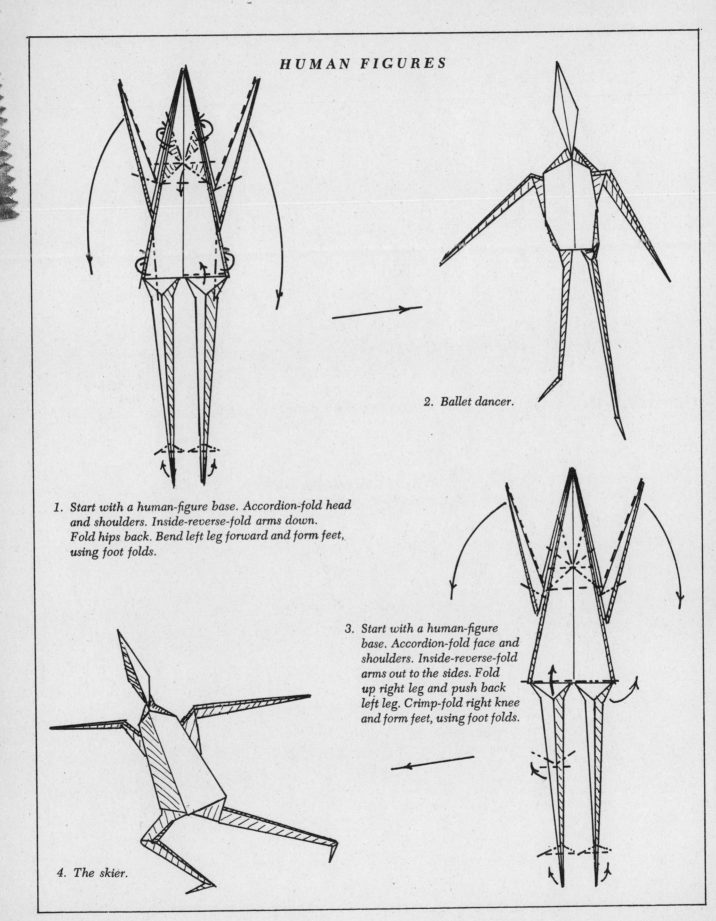

2. Ballet dancer.

1. Start with a human-figure base. Accordion-fold head and shoulders. Inside-reverse-fold arms down. Fold hips back. Bend left leg forward and form feet, using foot folds.

3. Start with a human-figure base. Accordion-fold face and shoulders. Inside-reverse-fold arms out to the sides. Fold up right leg and push back left leg. Crimp-fold right knee and form feet, using foot folds.

4. The skier.

# THE APE

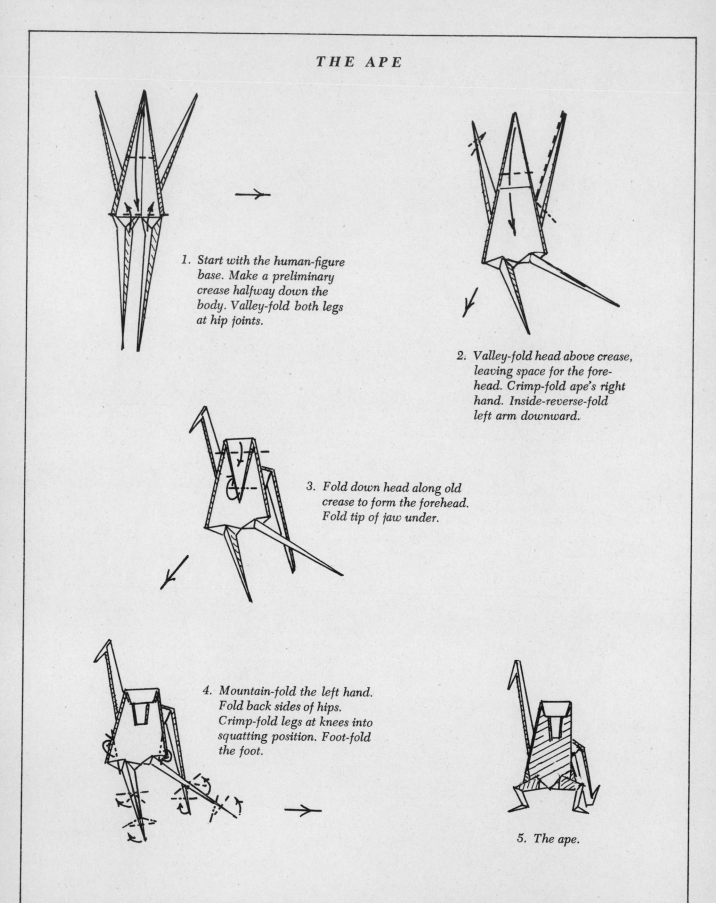

1. Start with the human-figure base. Make a preliminary crease halfway down the body. Valley-fold both legs at hip joints.

2. Valley-fold head above crease, leaving space for the forehead. Crimp-fold ape's right hand. Inside-reverse-fold left arm downward.

3. Fold down head along old crease to form the forehead. Fold tip of jaw under.

4. Mountain-fold the left hand. Fold back sides of hips. Crimp-fold legs at knees into squatting position. Foot-fold the foot.

5. The ape.

## THE CHERRY BLOSSOM

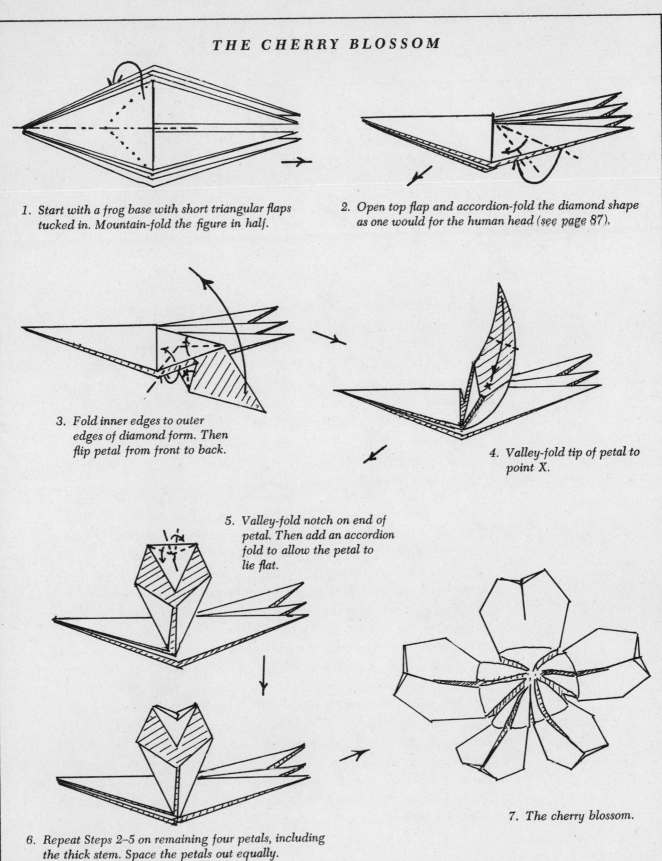

1. Start with a frog base with short triangular flaps tucked in. Mountain-fold the figure in half.

2. Open top flap and accordion-fold the diamond shape as one would for the human head (see page 87).

3. Fold inner edges to outer edges of diamond form. Then flip petal from front to back.

4. Valley-fold tip of petal to point X.

5. Valley-fold notch on end of petal. Then add an accordion fold to allow the petal to lie flat.

6. Repeat Steps 2–5 on remaining four petals, including the thick stem. Space the petals out equally.

7. The cherry blossom.

# CHAPTER XI

# The Offset Bird Base

The offsetting of the center point is probably the most important innovation I have to offer. It results in flaps of three unequal lengths, instead of the four of equal length in the bird or frog base. It is also possible to vary the degree of offset, if desired, to achieve flaps of different proportions. The flying crane can be made from a regular bird base, but the leg and the wings are of the same length and the neck is short. The offset-center base provides much more pleasing proportions; it is an excellent figure, by the way, to make a mobile. The offset center is also the secret of the staggered legs of my insects, which are not included in this volume.

The mask was designed after seeing Akira Yoshizawa's mask, which is made from a bird base. The staggered locations of the eyes, nose and mouth, offset the center frame and provide a suitable base. Obvious efforts have been made to achieve the desired effect instead of simply allowing the figure to adopt its own form. In order to form the nose, it was necessary to relieve the buckling tendency by means of an accordion fold in the back. The mouth also required taking up a slack on the sides of the face, which was then folded back along the sides. The eyes and the cheekbones, as well as the mouth, are made to cast a shadow, which gives the mask its effectiveness. Variations of the mask can be made by changing the degree of offset.

The offset eight-point star is folded as one would fold an eight-point star, with the exception that the starting position is the offset bird base. The result is not particularly attractive, but does produce points of unequal lengths. The difference in lengths of the points is used effectively in the dachshund. When it was originally made from an eight-point star, the resemblance was poor. The dachshund is related to the mouse in basic form.

# THE OFFSET BIRD BASE

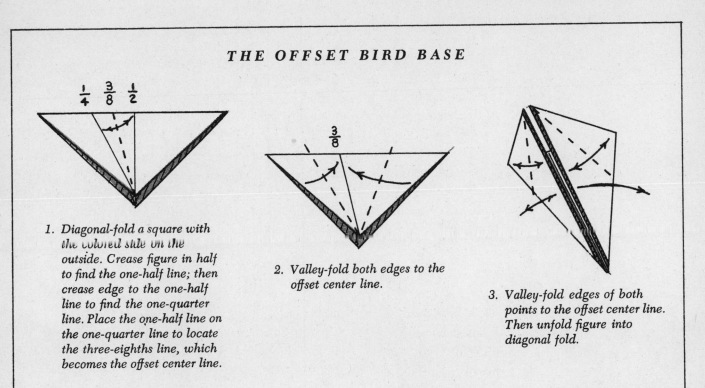

1. *Diagonal-fold a square with the colored side on the outside. Crease figure in half to find the one-half line; then crease edge to the one-half line to find the one-quarter line. Place the one-half line on the one-quarter line to locate the three-eighths line, which becomes the offset center line.*

2. *Valley-fold both edges to the offset center line.*

3. *Valley-fold edges of both points to the offset center line. Then unfold figure into diagonal fold.*

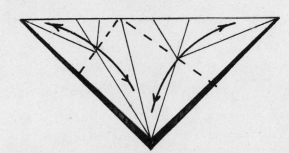

4. *Valley-fold upper edges to the offset center line. This completes the preliminary creases, which bisect the angles of the right and left flaps.*

5. *Inside-reverse-fold the right and left corners as one would for the square preliminary fold.*

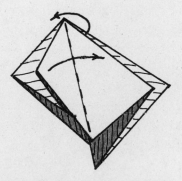

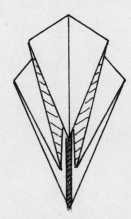

6. *Book-fold one front and one rear flap to rotate flaps.*

7. *Offset square fold: Using preliminary creases, inside-reverse-fold all four flaps.*

8. *The offset bird base.*

The Egyptian cat illustrates the usefulness of the staggered points. It is made from an offset bird base with a sunken point. The center "square" is opened up to form an X-form as one did for the fox. A cat made from a regular bird base would be shorter and less attractive.

I once made an owl from an offset-center base with lack of symmetry on the two sides. The head and the beak were tilted to one side, and it looked like a drunken owl or one of Picasso's figures. Lack of symmetry represents a dimension which remains to be explored more fully.

**THE OFFSET
EIGHT-POINT STAR**

**THE MASK**

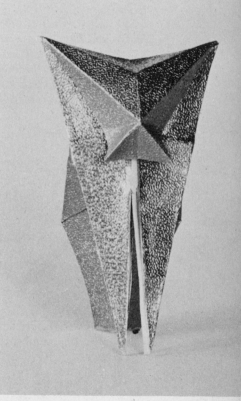

**THE EGYPTIAN CAT**

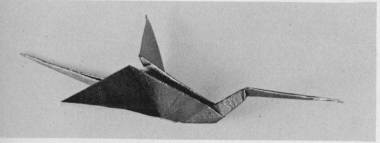

**THE FLYING CRANE**

**THE DACHSHUND**

## THE FLYING CRANE

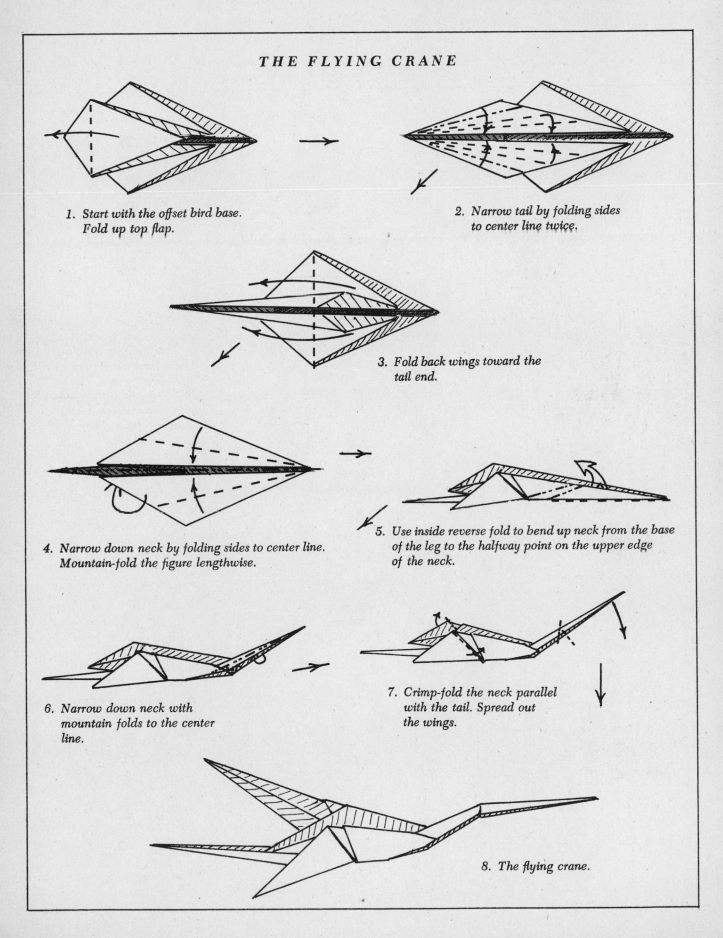

1. Start with the offset bird base. Fold up top flap.

2. Narrow tail by folding sides to center line twice.

3. Fold back wings toward the tail end.

4. Narrow down neck by folding sides to center line. Mountain-fold the figure lengthwise.

5. Use inside reverse fold to bend up neck from the base of the leg to the halfway point on the upper edge of the neck.

6. Narrow down neck with mountain folds to the center line.

7. Crimp-fold the neck parallel with the tail. Spread out the wings.

8. The flying crane.

# THE MASK

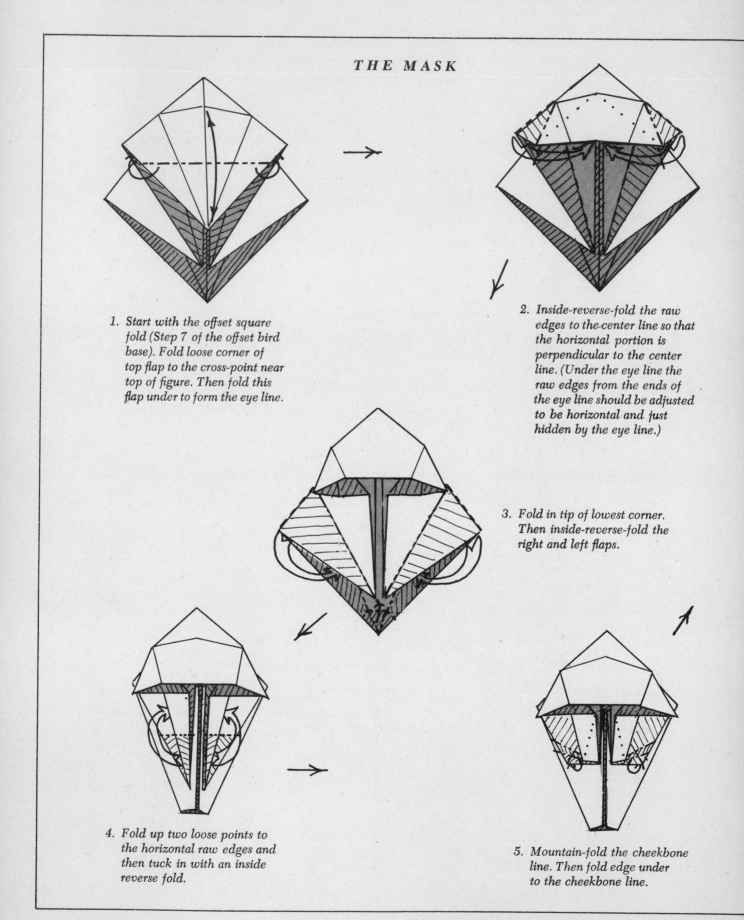

1. Start with the offset square fold (Step 7 of the offset bird base). Fold loose corner of top flap to the cross-point near top of figure. Then fold this flap under to form the eye line.

2. Inside-reverse-fold the raw edges to the center line so that the horizontal portion is perpendicular to the center line. (Under the eye line the raw edges from the ends of the eye line should be adjusted to be horizontal and just hidden by the eye line.)

3. Fold in tip of lowest corner. Then inside-reverse-fold the right and left flaps.

4. Fold up two loose points to the horizontal raw edges and then tuck in with an inside reverse fold.

5. Mountain-fold the cheekbone line. Then fold edge under to the cheekbone line.

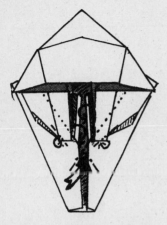

6. Open out figure. Mountain-fold two sheets under the nose along the dotted lines to lock in the nose to the sheet below it. Fold under corners of nose.

7. Fold cross-hatch sections under the nose and hold in place, because the figure will buckle. Turn it over.

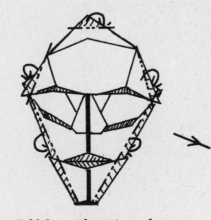

8. While holding the nose in place, accordion-fold the back to relieve the buckling tendency and to permit the figure to lie flat. Turn over to the front.

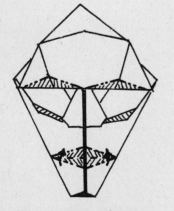

9. Make mountain-fold creases for the eyes. Then accordion-fold (mountain-valley-mountain) creases for the mouth. Fold lower mountain crease on top of the upper one to form the mouth.

10. Fold down edges of mouth to hold the mouth in place. Then extend edge fold along sides. Fold under sides and top of head.

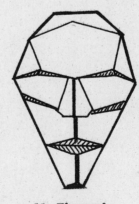

11. The mask.

# THE OFFSET EIGHT-POINT STAR

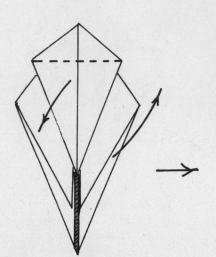

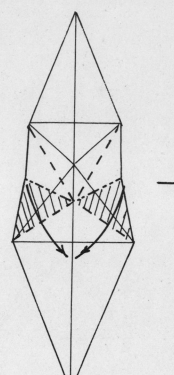

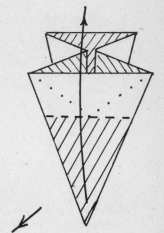

1. Start with the offset bird base. Pull apart the top and bottom flaps as far as they will go.

3. Sunken offset bird base. Valley-fold the large flap up even with hidden sunken point.

2. Sinking the center point: Push in sides and press down mountain fold (which forms of its own accord) along the center line. Mountain-fold the top and lower flaps.

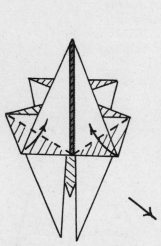

4. Fold in corners of folded flap.

5. Turn figure over.

6. Fold shortest flap so that its point meets those of the folded larger flap. Then fold in corners.

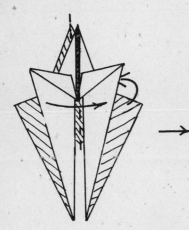

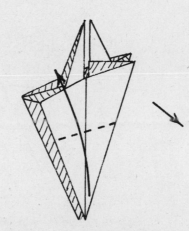

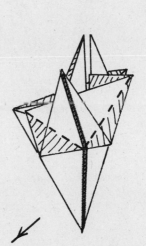

7. Rotate flaps by book-folding front and rear flaps.

8. Fold up intermediate-size flap as far as it will go, making it perpendicular to the upper edge rather than following the vertical center line.

9. Fold in corners of the folded flap. Repeat Steps 8 and 9 on reverse side.

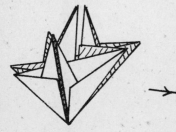

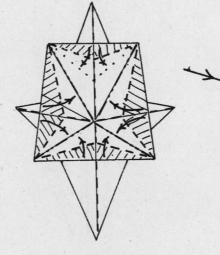

10. Flatten out figure, revealing center "square." Fold in four sides to diagonal lines. Press creases together and open up figure again.

12. The offset eight-point star.

11. Fold sides of center "square" to closest diagonal lines. Then press figure together into a star, following accordion folds.

# THE EGYPTIAN CAT

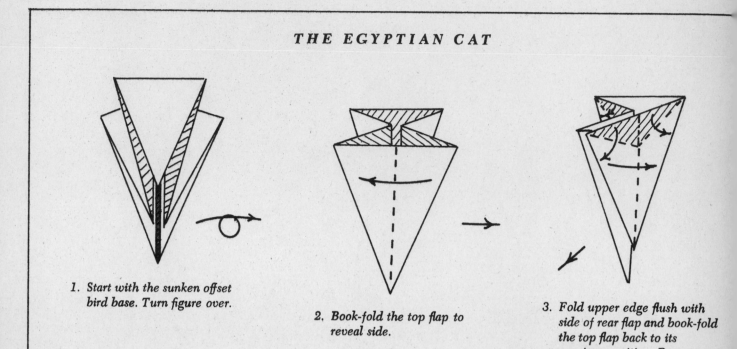

1. Start with the sunken offset bird base. Turn figure over.

2. Book-fold the top flap to reveal side.

3. Fold upper edge flush with side of rear flap and book-fold the top flap back to its previous position. Repeat on opposite side.

4. Valley-fold the lower flap up.

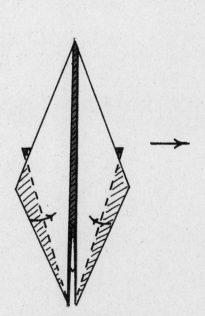

5. Valley-fold the sides of the legs even with reverse side.

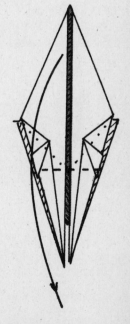

6. Fold down upper flap as far as it will go.

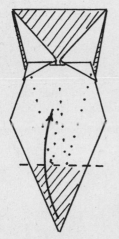

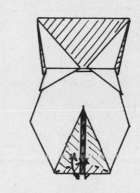

7. Fold up tail even with bottom of legs.

8. Fold up a notch on the bottom of the tail. Squeeze tail together and pull away from body at an angle. Fold sides of body together at right angle to each other.

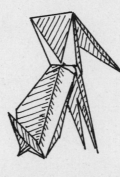

9. Turn figure over to the front.

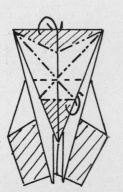

10. Make preliminary creases shown here. Then fold tip of point under. Mountain-fold the notch on top of the head to form ears. Use accordion folds to form catlike face.

11. The Egyptian cat.

# THE DACHSHUND

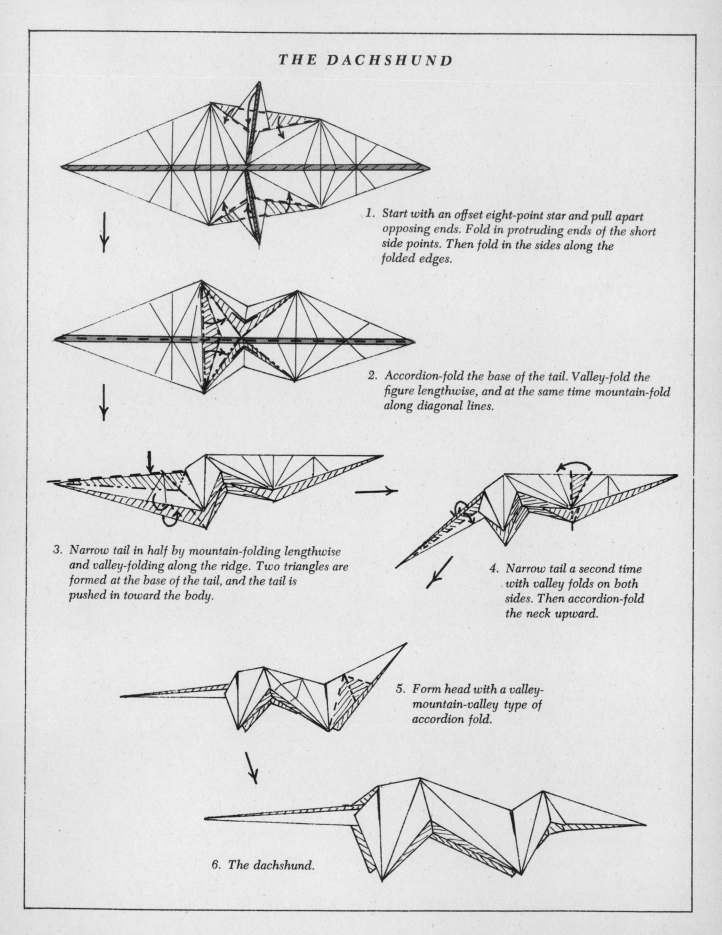

1. Start with an offset eight-point star and pull apart opposing ends. Fold in protruding ends of the short side points. Then fold in the sides along the folded edges.

2. Accordion-fold the base of the tail. Valley-fold the figure lengthwise, and at the same time mountain-fold along diagonal lines.

3. Narrow tail in half by mountain-folding lengthwise and valley-folding along the ridge. Two triangles are formed at the base of the tail, and the tail is pushed in toward the body.

4. Narrow tail a second time with valley folds on both sides. Then accordion-fold the neck upward.

5. Form head with a valley-mountain-valley type of accordion fold.

6. The dachshund.

## BIBLIOGRAPHY FOR ADULT PAPER FOLDING

Brossman, Julia and Martin. *A Japanese Paper Folding Classic* (excerpts from the *Kan no mado*). Washington, D.C.: Pinecone Press, 1961.

Harbin, Robert. *Secrets of Origami.* London: Old Bourne Book Company, 116 Fleet St., 1963.

Honda, Isao. *All about Origami.* Tokyo: Toto Bunka Co., 1960. Distributors: Japan Publications Trading Co., Central P.O. Box 722, Tokyo, Japan.

Kasahara, Kunihiko. *Origami o Tanoshimu Hon* (Let's Enjoy Origami). Kubo Shoten, 2-21 Matsugaoka, Nakanoku, Tokyo, Japan, 1966.

Mander, Jerry; Dippel, George; and Gossage, Howard. *The Great International Paper Airplane Book.* New York: Simon and Schuster, 1967.

Martin, Marie Gilbert. *Pasteless Construction with Paper.* New York: Pageant Press, 1951.

Murray, William D., and Rigney, Francis J. *Paper Folding for Beginners.* New York: Dover Press, 1960. (Recommended for traditional origami for beginners.)

Randlett, Samuel. *The Best of Origami.* New York: E. P. Dutton Co., 1961.

Solorzano Sagredo, Vincente. *Papiroflexia Zoomorfica.* Valladolid, Spain: 1962.

Uchiyama, Kosho. *Origami.* Kokudosha, Takata Toyokawa Cho, Bunkyo-Ku, Tokyo, Japan, 1962.

*1968 World Topic Yearbook,* pp. 78-79. Lake Bluff, Illinois: Tangley Oaks Educational Center, 1968.

Books on origami, subscriptions to the *Origamian* and supplies of origami paper may be obtained from the Origami Center, 71 West 11th Street, New York, New York 10011.

---

## SOURCE OF PACKAGED FOIL PAPER

It was the original intention of the author to have a pack of foil paper cut to size included with the book, but due to technical difficulties his plan was abandoned. Instead, arrangements have been made for preparation and distribution of packages of paper-backed foil separately. Foil paper, as indicated in the book, is superior to origami paper and is recommended for modern folders. The package consists of excellent quality foil paper 6½ inches square in a variety of colors and designs specially selected by the author.

---

J. C. Campbell Paper Company
30 Freight Street
Pawtucket, R.I. 02860

*(wholesale)*

Brown University Bookstore
Angell and Thayer Streets
Providence, R.I. 02912

*(retail and mail order: $1.00 per package)*

# *Indexes*

There are three indexes: an Index of Basic Forms, an Index of Basic Moves, and an Index of Figures. In the Index of Basic Moves, I have included cross references to a particular step in folding a figure. The number of the step is in parenthesis. A better notion of a move may be gained by examining several applications. Symbols and practice on them may be found on pages 22, 27, and 28.

## INDEX OF FIGURES

**ABOUT THE AUTHOR**

JAMES MINORU SAKODA was born in Lancaster, California. He was educated both in California and at Toyo University in Japan and received his Ph.D. from the University of California in 1949. Since that time, Dr. Sakoda has published over a dozen articles and is renowned as a social psychologist, statistician, and computer programmer. He is the winner of the Origami Division of the *Scientific American* Paper Airplane Contest held in 1967, and is currently a professor at Brown University. Dr. Sakoda lives in Barrington, Rhode Island, with his wife and their son, William, who attends Harvard University.